GENTLE JACK

THE DRAMA LIBRARY
General Editor: Edward Thompson

ROBERT BOLT

Gentle Jack

A Play in Two Acts

WITH AN INTRODUCTION BY

THE AUTHOR

HEINEMANN

Heinemann Educational Books Ltd
LONDON MELBOURNE TORONTO
SINGAPORE CAPE TOWN
AUCKLAND IBADAN
HONG KONG

First published 1965

Published by
Heinemann Educational Books Ltd
15-16 Queen Street, Mayfair, London W.1
Printed in Great Britain by
Bookprint Limited, Kingswood, Surrey

INTRODUCTION

I found the germ for *Gentle Jack* in the Jack-of-the-Green whose picture is on the cover of this book. His face, peering out of or withdrawing into the leaves which prove in fact to be part of his face, bears an expression at once gentle and ruthless, innocent and cynical, compassionate and perfectly indifferent. I do not see these opposite qualities instantaneously. But when I look at the face thinking it gentle the ruthless face emerges from it like an optical illusion to rebuke my sentimentalism. And no sooner have I accepted that the face is after all a ruthless face than the gentle face emerges to rebuke me for coarse moralizing. Obviously the face itself is not undergoing these alternations. It is merely I who cannot see opposites except as alternative. But the artist who carved the face, either because he lived when the world was younger or because he didn't deal in words but shapes and surfaces of stone, was somehow able to get them *together*. And I took his subject to be Nature – that world which we have risen above or fallen from but which still claims us, which we long for and fear.

We don't any longer call it that. The word 'Nature' has a compromised, Wordsworthian, irrelevantly rustic taint today. But we long for spontaneity, the quality we most admire and envy in animals. In art and in psychology (popular psychology at any rate) we value the unthought and the autonomous, we mistrust the calculated and purposive. On the other hand recent history and also our increasing honesty about our individual selves have shown that spontaneity is not always life-enhancing but can be squalid and fatal. Hence our ambivalent longing for and fear of Nature and 'Natural' qualities. All this and more seemed beautifully summed up in Jack-of-the-Green and I made him the occasion of my play.

It was performed by a superb cast led by Edith Evans and luminously directed by Noel Willman, but few of the critics liked my play and it attracted small audiences. Some found it over-obvious but mostly it was found obscure. So I am going to break the writer's golden rule and 'explain' what is meant to happen in it.

Miss Lazara is the representative of Man-outside-Nature, subject to government, awareness and judgment. She rules by the power of property. Property she has abstracted into money and money she has abstracted into figures. There is nothing physical in her life. She is unhappy but takes her position to be a privilege and a duty. Jacko is a natural man in headlong flight from Nature about which he knows too much. In Miss Lazara's empire he is recognized to be an alien, a refugee from some other realm, conforming desperately as refugees do but a source of discomfort and figure of fun to the true citizens. All the other humans in the play are citizens of Miss Lazara's empire, in high or low degree.

When Jacko is elected to be the pseudo-Jack an element of cruelty in the proceedings rouses the genuine article, Jack himself. He takes Jacko under his wing and they strike their bargain. Endowed with the power of Nature Jacko is able to do himself and the citizens of Miss Lazara's empire a lot of good. All are to some extent released and behave more spontaneously than they did. Even Miss Lazara at last succumbs, making a voluntary abdication of her power so as to satisfy her desire for Bilbo.

But the genuine Jack desires among other things murder. At this point Jacko draws back. But he does not retreat back into the empire of ordered society, he takes a Promethean stance. He will retain the gentle and liberating attributes of Nature while rejecting Nature's senseless destructiveness. He will be both free and moral, spontaneous and rational. The god is enraged and a struggle ensues. If you don't believe in wood gods, even in the theatre, then Jack and Jacko may be taken to be two halves of a split personality.

The god finds easily enough within the little empire sufficient resentment and brutality to secure the murder which he wants. At one point only does he seem likely to be checked. When at the climax Miss Lazara returns from the city with Bilbo in tow she reasserts her authority, loosening the grip of the god on her people and reducing the occasion to its proper insignificance. But a chance remark by one of her employees strikes her own Achilles' heel (her age and unlived life) and the god is roused in herself. Enraged she sacks her employees. But employment was the only bond which bound them; she exercised no sanctions of tradition or religion or superior morality, standing only on her rights as an employer. That bond gone her society is dissolved and the god takes over.

Morgan, the champion of the abstract, arch-enemy of Nature, is sacrificed. This is not the murder which the god desires because the god kills Morgan himself. Or, if you look at it the other way, Jacko kills Morgan while he is insane, and since insane not fully human. Morgan's death is merely the bait. The murder is accomplished when Jacko himself is killed by his fellow humans. The god would have preferred a proper ritual killing to this grubby but effective weapon of righteous indignation, but a murder is a murder and, satiated, he can go whence he came.

I suppose my conclusion was this: The world of pure reason and the world of pure impulse are alike uninhabitable by human beings. The only habitable world is one where some kind of compromise is achieved. But no compromise is possible. Where the two worlds meet and appear reconciled what has really happened is the secret surrender of one to the other. Hence our irreducible dissatisfaction. No truly habitable world exists.

I tried to persuade myself that the failure of the play to attract a sufficient audience might stem from the unpalatable nature of this conclusion, but I think the reason was simpler.

I do like plays in which the people have ideas as well as predicaments, but I think what happened with this play was that I became so interested in the ideas that the ideas rather than the people have the predicaments, clash, come to their climax, and so on. And I had a couple of aesthetic ideas to prosecute as well: something to do with the necessary unreality of theatrical characters as against real characters, and something to do with the Theatres of Cruelty and the Absurd. I wanted to put the Cruel in a gentle context and the Absurd in a reasonable context, because I thought that the Absurd in an absurd context would be like black writing on black paper – not even absurd, but nothing.

The play was meant to entertain. Indeed it was meant to be funny. But I think the audiences felt all the mere will and effort that went into the writing of it, and were repelled. Some love went into the writing too, but not enough.

A number of people, not all of them personal friends, did find it entertaining in performance. And I am very pleased that it can now be read.

ROBERT BOLT

GENTLE JACK

GENTLE JACK *was first presented in London at The Queen's Theatre on 28 November 1963 by H. M. Tennent Ltd, with the following cast:*

SECRETARY	Peter Wyatt
CHAMPION	A. J. Brown
VIOLET	Edith Evans
JACKO	Michael Bryant
BILBO	William Dexter
MORGAN	John Phillips
PENELOPE	Sian Phillips
HUBERT	Timothy West
TREADGOLD	Noel Howlett
MRS TREADGOLD	Edith Sharpe
GASTON	David Calderisi
CYNTHIA	Polly Adams
BRACKET	Barry Lineham
MRS BRACKET	Gretchen Franklin
GRIEVES	Bernard Kay
JACK	Kenneth Williams
OLD LABOURER	Peter Wyatt
YOUNG LABOURER	Erik Mason
COUNTRY SERVANTS	Michael Martin
	Ernest Jennings
	Barry Stanton
	Peter Tunstall

The Play directed by
NOEL WILLMAN

Scenery and costumes designed by
DESMOND HEELEY

Music by
CARL DAVIS

xi

CHARACTERS IN THE PLAY

CHAMPION: A City man approaching his retirement, say seventy. Everything about him, from his voice to his virtues, is tastefully restrained. In any conventional situation a tower of strength and delightful company.

VIOLET: Some dozen years younger than Champion, graceful, gracious, beautifully dressed. Wayward but unvaryingly successful. Her charm is profound, her anger truly dangerous. She can be by turns delicately gentle and shockingly coarse. Riches and power she takes as a matter of course, having never been without them.

JACKO: About thirty. A knotty strength constricted in an ill-cut humbleness. Aggressively placating, importunately self-effacing, magnetic without knowing it, he is a man no-one can leave alone, a natural butt.

BILBO: The same age as Jacko, but there resemblance ends. His behaviour is so felicitous that it would signal calculation in anyone less fresh, sanguine and unforcedly charming. He is ambitious and has the wit not to conceal it – seems born for success.

MORGAN: About fifty. Too scrupulous for natural satisfaction, cultivating stillness, by nature sympathetic, he attracts affection from which he can derive no benefit. An intellectual of the first water. His vanity survives in the perfection of his manner.

PENELOPE: Late twenties. A fine animal. She has taken everything that offered but found it not enough. Hence a conscious harshness in her voice, a quality of brooding clouding her vitality, as a fine animal balked.

HUBERT: A middle-aged labourer. Congenitally half-witted,

thick of speech and body, he is painful when he attempts ordinary intercourse, but has arbitrary moments of authority, gone as quickly as they come.

TREADGOLD: About sixty. A little, birdlike, naturally happy, easily disturbed man, loving agreement, hating friction. An excellent priest to conduct the decent dying of a country parish.

MRS TREADGOLD: His consort, and physically like him. A fresh-skinned village woman not without good sense, but timid, her life has been a series of small charities and charity is now the only meaning of her life, with him as its centre.

GASTON: An athletic young Frenchman and man of the world. Gravely gay, softly masculine, marvellously well-balanced, he makes life seem simpler than it can be to the Anglo-Saxons who surround him.

CYNTHIA: A rich girl of twenty. Well educated but not clever; vital and privileged; greedy but not mean. Her manner is her mother's but inside it is a child.

BRACKET: Middle forties. A physically uncouth, modest man accustomed to hard work, and healthy. Within his work mature and masterful, beyond it something of a youth.

MRS BRACKET: Early forties, a childless wife. While her husband has been working she has brought to bear on all the tenderest places of her mind a lot of clumsy probity and half-digested information.

GRIEVES: A very serious, very formidable, class-conscious worker. He is a Puritan, giving no quarter as a matter of duty. He is responsible for himself, which sets him apart, a leader, biding his time.

JACK: Of no age; a pandering urchin, infinitely irresponsible; a fallen god suffering and withdrawn. A liar and a teacher, a murderer and a benefactor, he is finally impersonal, like a cold wind. His charm is absolute, but to himself all human contact is an ignoble imposition and painful charade.

Also: SECRETARY, CLERKS, HOUSE-SERVANTS, LABOURERS.

A NOTE ON THE SETTING

The action of the play takes place at Miss Violet Lazara's city offices and in the Forest of Attis Abbey, one of her country residences.

Emptiness and bright light are the main components of the Office Set. The table and stool should be in the best of the most modern taste. The Jacobean 'throne' to be a beauty. Nothing else.

The Forest Set will have to have more presence of its own. Apart from the picture of Attis Abbey it will consist of foliage. This should be capable of thickening swiftly and should convey an *impression* of leafiness, be able to sway, billow, be pushed aside. Above all this Set should be responsive to changes of light. In bright light it should be transparent and liberating, in shadow opaque and enclosing. In short it must be like a forest, and I don't think this can be achieved by imitation trees.

A NOTE ON THE MUSIC

However it is done the effect should be that the Bees, though recognizably insectile, are people. People in a different world from ours of course, the unguessable world of nature which their voices tell us is fiercer and sweeter than our own world, hence alluring, but since it isn't our world also frightening.

ACT ONE

A modern City chamber represented by a single huge window occupying the rear of the stage. 'Behind' this window a block of offices, netted in scaffolding, being reared against the sky. Very designed furniture represented by a table comprising a slab of glass on four steel prongs, a stool in the same mode, and behind the table a Jacobean carved oak chair – almost a throne. A SECRETARY *in a city suit is preparing a pile of large, thick coloured cards on the table, watched by* CHAMPION, *who reaches forward, adjusts something to his own satisfaction, then comes downstage and addresses the audience.* SECRETARY *all the time busy behind him.*

CHAMPION: My name is Champion and I am as it were Chief Secretary of State to a considerable Empire. I am Miss Violet Lazara's Director of Accounts.

Our assets in round figures are: (*he recites just too fast to follow*) twenty-five millions of real estate, twelve and-a-half million gilt-edged stock, nineteen million industrials, nine millions in municipal bonds mostly South American. Please keep count. I am reducing rupees, roubles, lira, dollars, deutschmarks, yen, to pounds for your convenience – five millions in short term loans. We have controlling interests in Trading Trusts with Active Assets of say thirty millions and a half. The total, for anybody slow, is one hundred and one millions.

SECRETARY *comes forward and hands the cards to* CHAMPION, *then goes back to the table.*

From time to time we handle bullion, we are our own

discounting house, our holding company has a trading fund which . . . we do not disclose.

All this, Miss Lazara possesses.

Enter VIOLET. *She crosses and sits in the chair, held for her by* SECRETARY, *watched smilingly by* CHAMPION, *who turns back to audience and continues:*

Did she make it? No, she has it by inheritance. But she also has inherited ability. She is a lady with a mind.

He joins VIOLET *and* SECRETARY *at the table and a ritual commences. He places the cards before her one by one. She makes her comment and slides each card to the left in a mounting pile.* SECRETARY *records her decision on a long strip of paper.*

Austrian Bank of Commerce.

VIOLET: Nothing.

CHAMPION: Michelin Rubber.

VIOLET: Nothing.

CHAMPION: Cardboard Boxes.

VIOLET: Nothing.

CHAMPION: Iranian Silver.

VIOLET: Iranian Silver looks well this morning?

CHAMPION: Yes indeed.

She places that card to the right.

Treasury two and a half.

VIOLET: Nothing.

CHAMPION: Treasury two and three quarters.

VIOLET: Nothing.

CHAMPION: Egyptian Metals.

VIOLET: What's the matter with Egyptian Metals?

CHAMPION: From this morning's *New York Times.*

He puts before her a press cutting mounted on a card.

VIOLET: Ah . . . We'll *buy* Egyptian Metals.

CHAMPION: Buy, Madam? They're very pale, really quite sickly.

VIOLET: Yes and we shall go on buying them until – Iranian Silver looks less robust.

She hands both cards and cutting to CHAMPION *with a suggestion of triumph. He glances through them, murmuring.*

CHAMPION: Ah yes . . . yes of course. However, what we gain upon the swings we shall have lost upon the roundabouts shall we not?

VIOLET: Not necessarily. Cable.

CHAMPION *snaps his fingers.*

SECRETARY *takes shorthand.*

The Chairman, Imperial Enterprise, Imperial House, Pittsburg – My dear Rothschild, We have received your cable. We avail ourselves your option as of noon this date and thank you. I intend transfer via Basle, Tangier, Hong Kong. Suggest you leak this Wall Street Wednesday after close of Change. Glorious weather here. I leave this morning for the country and return next week, till when we hold ourselves contracted in the terms your letter of the——

CHAMPION: Twelfth.

VIOLET: Twelfth. Well?

CHAMPION: Oh very neat. Impeccable. If it *is* Imperial.

VIOLET: Of course it's Imperial.

CHAMPION: The figures indicate it, certainly.

VIOLET: The figures. Intuition, Champion.

CHAMPION: Yes Madam.

VIOLET: *Womanly* intuition.

CHAMPION: Yes Madam.

VIOLET: Then congratulate me!

CHAMPION: Oh I do. Upon your knowledge of the figures. (*He leaves her and comes forward as before.*) Perhaps you ask if either – birth or brains, in a world so largely poor can justify possession of so much? That kind of question makes the thorny crown of the philosopher, which we do not usurp. It is so. As molecules make matter so money comes together into empires. We have the crown of gold. Which presses hard enough. And has made many another queen, a virgin. And so it is with her.

VIOLET: Mr Champion!

CHAMPION (*approaching*): Madam?

VIOLET: There is neither letter nor cable from Mexico?

CHAMPION and SECRETARY exchange a glance, quickly suppressed.

CHAMPION: No.

VIOLET: You hesitate?

CHAMPION: No Madam, there is neither letter nor cable.

VIOLET: The young man takes a high hand.

CHAMPION: Yes Madam.

VIOLET: He carries himself . . . confidently, the young man.

CHAMPION: It becomes him to.

VIOLET: You say so to please me.

He simpers, the smile whips from her face.

It does *not* please me! The young man is not my son – though I am 'old enough to be his mother'. He is an employee!

CHAMPION (*hastily*): Chase Manhattan.

VIOLET: Nothing.

Enter JACKO. SECRETARY looks at him but neither VIOLET nor CHAMPION seems aware of his presence as they continue the ritual. JACKO meanwhile hovers just on stage. His boots squeak softly.

CHAMPION: Banque Nationale Belgique.

VIOLET: Nothing.

CHAMPION: Banque Nationale Suisse.

VIOLET: Nothing.

CHAMPION: Pacific Irrigation.

VIOLET: Who is *hovering*?

SECRETARY (*to CHAMPION*): Mr Cadence.

CHAMPION: Mr Cadence.

VIOLET: Jacko Cadence, what do you want?

JACKO (*eagerly and ridiculously proffering a thin folder from the far side of the stage*): It's the Abstract on the Clough-Duff merger. I've done it.

VIOLET: You should not come in here until I've finished with the figures!

He makes to go.

Stay now! Show me.

He sets off towards her.

You still have not done anything about your boots!

He stops dead, stranded.

Show me!

He approaches hastily, and gives it to her. She gives it her attention.

In the silence, he says to her, with stupid sang-froid:

JACKO: Good morning!

Silence.

(*To* CHAMPION, *more quietly.*) Good morning.

Silence.

(*To* SECRETARY, *softly.*) Good morning.

SECRETARY *smiles faintly. Silence.* JACKO *coughs, covers his mouth, knocks the pile of cards onto the floor.*

VIOLET: Oh clumsy!

He goes down after them. She watches him grovel.

You are clumsy, Jacko!

JACKO: I'm sorry!

VIOLET: Clumsy and tentative!

JACKO: I'm sorry.

VIOLET: It's a sorry combination in a man.

He puts the cards back on the table, she watching darkly.

How is it you distract me?

JACKO: I've reduced it all to figures (*the folder*).

CHAMPION: He has made the figures very beautifully.

JACKO: Thank you.

VIOLET: Too beautifully. Like a copy clerk.

JACKO: I'm sorry.

VIOLET: Did you work at home? At night?

JACKO: Yes I did.

VIOLET: Don't. Nothing you can do for me is worth a young man's evenings.

JACKO: I'm sorry.

She tears the folder across and across.

VIOLET: The Clough–Duff merger's fallen through, Jacko. British Petroleum opted last night. You've been wasting your time. You have no luck! Champion.

CHAMPION *deftly places the remaining five cards in a row before her.*

Nothing. Nothing. Nothing. Nothing. Oh . . . bullion.

She picks up the last card. It is golden. All of them – even, after a pause, JACKO – bend towards it as though drawn physically. I shall want a background for this, Mr Champion. Can one of the young men make me a background?

CHAMPION: Young Westminster is in Budapest . . . Young Lloyd and Barclay Junior will not be back from Stockholm till tomorrow . . . Mr Cadence seems to be free?

VIOLET: Oh Jacko can't do bullion. This wants someone with a very sharp blade indeed. One slip with this, Mr Champion, and we might easily lose a limb. Indeed, if he were not in Mexico, I would say this wanted Bilbo Cubit.

Enter BILBO.

VIOLET *stares, turns away, takes off her pince-nez.*

BILBO: Good morning Violet. Good morning Jacko Cadence. Did somebody say 'bullion'?

VIOLET: Good morning Bilbo. I thought you were in Mexico.

BILBO: It's very hot in Mexico. I have returned.

VIOLET: I do see that. Did I send for you?

BILBO: No. It's a surprise.

VIOLET: And does Signor Santa Cruz want to buy my hotels?

BILBO *(scribbles on a piece of paper before her, with an elegant silver pencil)*: That's his figure.

VIOLET: That's very good; we'll take it.

BILBO: I have done.

VIOLET: You have sold my hotels?

BILBO: For that figure.

VIOLET: It's a very good figure indeed. You must have been clever.

BILBO: Clever . . . ? No, but industrious. Every day for three weeks I have been to the bull-fight. Signor Santa Cruz is devoted to the bulls.

VIOLET: Why didn't you cable, Bilbo?

BILBO: I wanted to see you.

VIOLET: It's a little high-handed.

BILBO: I know. I should have cabled. But I thought: 'I've done a good job of work for her; now it's time for pleasure.' (*He puts his hand on hers.*) So I came.

VIOLET: Could you find no 'pleasures' in Mexico City?

BILBO: Only the bull-fight.

VIOLET: Oh, I have no right to ask you——!

BILBO: Only the bull-fight.

VIOLET: Poor Bilbo! Every day – for three weeks?

    BILBO, SECRETARY *and* CHAMPION *smile. Fun is toward.*

BILBO: Oh I tell you I've been working. The heat! And the enthusiasm! I was required to salivate, visibly, when the horn went in – it does go in you know, one sees it quite plainly. How it goes in. And where it goes in!

VIOLET: Where does it go in?

BILBO: Oh I couldn't tell you – not in front of Jacko.

VIOLET: Jacko's blushing——

BILBO: What is it, Jacko——?

CHAMPION: No I protest, you shan't bait Mr Cadence.

BILBO: But why's he blushing——?

CHAMPION: I deny the blush——

SECRETARY: It's true, sir, he *is* blushing.

CHAMPION: Then I applaud the blush – the blush is delicate——

VIOLET: – It's true!

BILBO: – The very word!

VIOLET: – He's delicate!

They have passed from smiles, to giggles, to laughter, and their laughter is not sneering but good hearted. With a sudden movement JACKO *huddles himself protectively over the paper as though avoiding blows, and at this they become helpless.*

BILBO: – What's he got there?

VIOLET: – Figures——!

CHAMPION: He does make exquisite figures——!

VIOLET: – He has a special pen——!

Their laughter in crescendo becomes a disciplined harsh barking. HA HA HA HA HA HA HA – *and at once dies away and they approach him, feeling kindly.*

CHAMPION: You should refute them Cadence, really you should.

SECRETARY: You'll be the death of some of us Mr Cadence, really you will.

BILBO: All work and no play makes Jacko a dull boy. Let's have a look . . .

He takes the golden card from under JACKO's *reluctant fingers, comes downstage and holds it up, absorbed. At once the muffled giggling of* SECRETARY *is cut off, the smile goes from* CHAMPION's *face and both glance apprehensively at* VIOLET, *who stops dead.* BILBO, *becoming aware of the silence and stillness, turns.*

(*To* VIOLET, *politely, waving card.*) May I?

VIOLET: Certainly.

BILBO (*is again absorbed*): How much have we got?

VIOLET: I've got half a million ounces.

BILBO: *Have* we now . . . ? I wonder what it looks like . . . I wonder what it is in tons . . .

Unnoticed, JACKO *begins to scribble.*

Have you ever seen any bullion, Violet?

VIOLET: No.

BILBO: Don't you want to?

VIOLET: No.

BILBO: Truly? You never want, actually . . . to put your hands on it . . . ?

VIOLET: No. Do you?

BILBO: Yes; I think it's natural.

VIOLET: It's vulgar. I also own a lot of land; should I therefore learn to plough?

BILBO laughs appreciatively and returns to her. Catching her still cold and regal gaze:

BILBO: Oh you're right, obviously. (*He puts down the card, saying easily*) I'll do it.

VIOLET: Make me a background.

BILBO: Of course, but I'll do it too. Shall I?

VIOLET: I'll do it.

BILBO: I can.

VIOLET: Undoubtedly. I taught you.

BILBO: Pff – There's nothing to it.

VIOLET: No?

BILBO: No. (*Pointing to card.*) There's the enemy . . . There and there. Follow the advance and lead the retreat – that's all it comes to.

VIOLET: I'll do it!

BILBO: Why?

VIOLET: It's mine!

JACKO: It's thirteen tons, nineteen hundredweights, no quarters, two pounds.

BILBO (*irritable*): What?

JACKO: Half a million ounces . . .

BILBO: Why not let *him* make you a background?

VIOLET (*sweetly*): What a good idea. Mr Cadence, will you make me a background?

JACKO: Oh. Yes. Thank you. (*To* BILBO.) Thank you.

He reaches for the card but BILBO *slams his own hand on it.*

VIOLET: What interesting hands you both have. Your hands are rather feminine, Bilbo.

BILBO: I do assure you they are not.

    JACKO *removes his hand; instantly,* BILBO *is gracious.*

BILBO: All right, Jacko, have a try.

JACKO: Thank you.

VIOLET: Thank you Mr Champion.

    CHAMPION *and* SECRETARY *bow and withdraw, but when they are extreme Stage Right:*

Mr Champion!

    CHAMPION *stops and turns.*

    SECRETARY *proceeds off.*

    VIOLET *joins* CHAMPION *and draws him extreme downstage.* BILBO *and* JACKO *do nothing; the convention is they cannot hear.*

Mr Champion, you knew that Mr Cubit had returned, did you not?

CHAMPION: I must confess I did.

VIOLET: Yet when I asked if you had heard from Mexico you said that you had not.

CHAMPION: You asked if there were letter or cable from Mexico, and I said that there was not.

VIOLET: A – a – ah . . . (*roguishly.*) You prevaricated!

CHAMPION: The young man wanted to surprise you. I ventured to suppose the surprise would be a pleasant one.

VIOLET: You did.

CHAMPION (*belatedly alarmed*): Er, yes.

VIOLET: Mr Champion, you know more of my affairs than anyone, myself included. You were the foreman builder of my father's fortunes. You must acquaint yourself with my affairs in every detail to the end that you may calculate what profits and what losses I may make. You may be devious in that. You may advise, you may instruct me, in that. But if you wind yourself into me to the end that you may know me and to calculate my *mind*—— by God I'll sack you!

CHAMPION: Madam, madam . . .

VIOLET: You understand exactly what danger you are in?

CHAMPION: Yes, Madam, yes.

VIOLET: And the grounds of it?

CHAMPION: Yes!

VIOLET: Because I could not bear to lose you. Nor could my concerns.

She takes his hand; gratefully, he stoops over hers.

CHAMPION: Madam.

Exit CHAMPION.

VIOLET turns to JACKO and BILBO, bringing them back to 'life'.

BILBO: He's going to do the figures, and I'll tell him what they mean.

JACKO: I could have the figures done by Monday, Madam——

VIOLET: Oh no – No figures in the country. We are going into the country, Bilbo.

BILBO: Oh splendid!

VIOLET: You, I am afraid, are going back to Mexico.

BILBO (*level*): Am I Violet? What for?

VIOLET: To buy back my hotels.

BILBO: When?

VIOLET: Now. Today. At once. And then to sell them. But this time, when I tell you to sell them.

BILBO: You realize I shall have to top his figure – which is already more than they are worth.

VIOLET: I know you will be clever.

BILBO: Even if I am, it's a pretty expensive gesture.

VIOLET: No Bilbo, you made a gesture; I am establishing a fact.

BILBO: Violet, I adore you! (*Bending over her hand.*) Mm? Je t'adore.

No response.

Well then, to Mexico.

Withdrawing backwards, sees JACKO hunched on his stool.

I do leave you in very safe hands.

VIOLET: Oh, Jacko is a different man at Attis Abbey.

JACKO (*alarmed*): Attis Abbey? Are we going to Attis Abbey?

VIOLET: Yes.

JACKO: No thank you.

> BILBO *laughs softly*.

VIOLET: Jacko, I'm inviting you to be my guest.

JACKO: Not at Attis Abbey!

VIOLET : Then bring your work, and come because I tell you to. The property's mine. Your father is dead. You'll come to no harm.

> *She and* BILBO, JACKO *dismissed from mind, confront each other midstage, with softened glances.*

BILBO: You're going to miss me.

VIOLET: Yes. Be quick.

> *He goes, but turns.*

BILBO: Mexico, in Midsummer?

VIOLET: If I could make it snow for you, I would. But go you shall.

> *They turn about, she going Stage Left, he Stage Right, where he stops and addresses the audience.*

BILBO: Twenty years ago I suppose she was 'a fascinating bitch'; now she's – less fascinating. Yes I know. (*He is not sharing a joke with them, but coldly correcting them for a vulgar error.*) She's rich though. And our noses, tongues, and other appendages are not more personal than our balance in the Bank – ask anybody poor. She's not uncomely. Beautifully clean. And rich. It's my belief that opulence unclothed might even be exciting; might be magnificent.

> *Exit* BILBO.

> VIOLET *speaks*.

VIOLET: He'll catch the 'plane tonight; tomorrow night he will be ... Where? 'The bull-fight'? Hardly ... But wherever, he'll be there because I sent him; I've won again ... But a woman who wins, who always wins, is that a woman?

(*She contemplates her own body.*) Oh yes, that's a woman. And an old one. With not much time to learn the posture of defeat. And that time bought with money. Good grief, my body knows the trick already – merely sleep defeats my body every night! But to make my *mind* fall backwards . . . He'll be naked somewhere . . . in some room . . . in some garden . . . under trees . . . some music playing . . . or whatever else it is they do. And I'll be at my country 'property' well clothed, very well clothed. (*With startling venom at motionless* JACKO.) With you, you pitiable thing!

Exit VIOLET.

At once the music of the insects is heard and JACKO *looks on fearfully, as:*

(1) SECRETARY *and* CLERKS *enter, take office furniture and go.*

(2) COUNTRY SERVANTS *enter with garden furniture and go.*

(3) MORGAN *enters with a book and sits.*

(4) *A large picture of* ATTIS HALL, *middle distance, replaces the 'window' of the office.*

(5) FOLIAGE *is flown in.*

JACKO *takes off his jacket for the heat and mops his brow. He sits crouched over his papers and looks after* VIOLET. MORGAN *follows his gaze.*

MORGAN: She's feeling guilty.

JACKO: *Violet?*

MORGAN: Guilty.

JACKO *is amazed and fascinated but on this word the* MUSIC *stops. His head jerks up. He gazes into the leaves above, fearfully.*

JACKO: Listen.

MORGAN: What?

JACKO: The bees have stopped.

MORGAN: So they have. Why do they do that?

JACKO: I don't know. They do . . . (*desperately*) Why does she bring me here?

MORGAN: She's feeling guilty.

JACKO: *Why?*

MORGAN: Because she killed your father, Jacko.

JACKO: She took his estate; that's happened before.

MORGAN: She took his estate and it killed him.

JACKO: Well . . .

MORGAN: And she's afraid of death.

JACKO: She's not.

MORGAN: Not——?

JACKO: Not afraid of death.

    MORGAN *laughs a gentle laugh of pure amusement.*

She's not; she's not afraid of anything.

    MORGAN *laughs as before.*

She's a great woman!

MORGAN: Very well if that's the way you want her.

    He is about to address himself to his book.

JACKO: I know what you all think about my father – you think he was left over from the Giant Time. I'll tell you about my father. He despised women. He was good with a gun. He thought he'd make an easy killing on the market – off Violet! (*He gains courage, and begins to exhibit a nasty small boy's glee.*) You should *see* what he bought and what he sold! A baby could have done better! A baby! (*But the conscious daring with which he shouts this into the trees shows him still afraid of his dead parent.*) He was a fool!

MORGAN: A great man, the great woman says.

JACKO: I mean a fool with money.

MORGAN: Ah. And you?

JACKO: I'm all right.

MORGAN: You don't give that impression.

JACKO: I mean I'm good with money.

MORGAN: Violet's money.

JACKO: I mean good with figures.

MORGAN: As a mathematician, I can hardly think so.

JACKO: Oh? Then why does she employ me?

MORGAN: She's feeling guilty.

JACKO (*approaching, incredulous fascination*): Did she *say* so?

MORGAN: Oh, she doesn't know.

    JACKO *starts away.*

  What's the matter?

JACKO: If she *heard* us talk like this——

MORGAN: Yes?

JACKO: She'd sack us!

MORGAN: She isn't my employer, She's my . . . (*chooses the word with self-mocking delicacy*) patron.

JACKO: She'd sack me.

MORGAN: And would no other House employ you?

JACKO (*looks away, shakes head, ashamed*): No.

MORGAN (*quite kindly*): Despite your gift for figures?

JACKO: I love the City, Dr Morgan.

MORGAN: Do you think so?

JACKO: I mean the City suits me!

MORGAN: My poor deluded lad.

JACKO: I mean I'm happy there!

MORGAN: How would *you* know that?

JACKO: Oh why can nobody leave me alone?

    A silence.

MORGAN: Violet's going to give you Attis Abbey.

JACKO: I wouldn't take it.

MORGAN: Are you sure? The trees are worth a lot of money.

JACKO: And I hate every leaf. And every insect. I hate the smell of leaves and the sound of insects. When I was a little boy once I dug a grave in the Forest, for my father, which I told him was a bear-trap. When I told him that he thought I'd got the right idea and I had a gamekeeper to help me. The soil there's very soft. Leaf mould. Dead leaves, dead fruits, anything dead, corrupted into soil by worms that live in it and won't take 'no' for an answer. It's centuries deep and, naturally, fertile. If I were Violet I'd have scooped it up with machines and sold!

  I hate every item in the schedule; mists and muck, hard

horn wet orifice, the skyline and the greasy pail, dung, hung game, cattle giving birth and being killed, the workers and their wives, sharp knives, stags, stallions, the whole extreme rude cruel way my father lived! But most of all I hate those trees, that stand there – Do you know he could have saved himself by cutting down those trees!

MORGAN: He must have loved them.

JACKO: He worshipped them!

MORGAN: Jacko.

JACKO: What?

MORGAN: Penelope Pelham is watching you.

JACKO (*instantly subdued*): Where?

MORGAN: On the edge of the Forest.

JACKO: What's she doing?

MORGAN: She's picking flowers for the King.

JACKO: Yes, would be doing that. (*He begins to gather his papers. Determinedly*) I'm going into the house.

MORGAN: Jacko, why?

JACKO: Because I've got important work to do.

MORGAN: Important?

JACKO: Oh no not important, only bullion, that's all, not a bit important.

And now to increase his agitation a gentle breeze begins to blow from the Forest, stirring the foliage and threatening to seize his papers.

MORGAN: Jacko, go and talk to her.

JACKO: Really, everybody seems to think he knows what's in me better than I know myself. It's amusing. Everyone urging me this way and that. It quite makes me laugh.

As he says this he goes for his jacket; the wind rising – and the INSECT MUSIC *coming with it – distributes his papers about the stage.* MORGAN *laughs, quite good-naturedly at first but quickly less so, at this climax to his confusion.*

MORGAN: Ha ha ha ha ha ha ha!

JACKO: Oh damn, damn, damn!

He is near to tears, and MORGAN *immediately sympathetic, slips from his seat to help him. Together they grovel for the papers, wind and music dying.*

MORGAN: Here.

JACKO: Dr Morgan you're very kind. And I value that, you know. I value that in people more than anything.

MORGAN (*soothing*): Gently, Jacko.

JACKO: No. No. You, are the kindest man I ever met.

MORGAN: You've been unlucky.

On the heels of the wind, unseen by either, PENELOPE *has entered. She stands immediately behind* JACKO, *so that* MORGAN, *handing his share of the papers to* JACKO – *both still crouching – sees her. He says, firmly:*

MORGAN: Now, Penelope, be sensible.

JACKO *spins round on his heels. This brings his face a few inches from her navel and he cannons back into* MORGAN *and both go sprawling.*

(*Furiously*) Jacko, be sensible!

PENELOPE (*cutting off her laughter; contrite*): Dr Morgan, are you all right?

MORGAN (*rising*): Yes thank you, perfectly.

JACKO *is still sitting where he sprawled.* PENELOPE *begins to gather the papers. She speaks with deep laughter beneath her voice, but quite gently.*

PENELOPE: Sorry Jacko, did I startle you?

JACKO (*at once emboldened to be vicious*): Just leave them alone will you! Just . . . leave them alone! It doesn't seem a lot to ask.

In stooping for the papers she has turned, accidentally or by design presenting her derrière.

You're horrible! Horrible!

She straightens and looks at him stonily.

You are a cruel, unpleasant girl!

PENELOPE (*softly*): Oh all right. Pick the bloody things up yourself.

C

Turns away, sits, her shoulder touching his jacket.

JACKO: I want my coat!

Indifferently she shrugs, defiantly he approaches. As he reaches for it she whips the garland over his head and takes a turn round his neck.

PENELOPE: You don't want *more* clothes, Jacko. You want less.

JACKO: I'll break it, Penelope!

PENELOPE: Unbutton, Jacko . . .

Holding the ends of the garland in one hand she begins to unbutton the waistcoat of his City suit with the other. He breaks the garland and runs to go, but with a bound enter HUBERT, *who bars his way.*

JACKO (*uncertainly, but with a smile of considerable charm*): Hello, Hubert.

HUBERT *regards him, motionless and silent.*

PENELOPE: Hey Hubert, don't you know him?

HUBERT *the same.*

JACKO. How are you Hubert?

HUBERT *thrusts out his hand.*

Oh no. (*With a little laugh he puts his hand behind him.*)

HUBERT *looks puzzled at his own palm as if to find there the cause of this discourtesy.*

Once bitten, twice shy, Hubert.

HUBERT *wipes his palm vigorously on his seat, and holds it out again.*

You'll hurt me.

HUBERT: 'Tis clean as 't'ever will be.

JACKO *puts his hand in* HUBERT's.

HUBERT *crushes it and pandemonium breaks out, thus:*

HUBERT (*bouncing up and down, feet thudding, bells chiming*): Hello Young Master Jack! Hello Young Master Jack! (*Ad lib.*)

PENELOPE (*overlapping*): Seize him Hubert! Seize him boy – good dog! (*Ad lib.*)

MORGAN (*overlapping*): Hubert behave yourself! Hubert behave yourself! (*Ad lib.*)

JACKO (*overlapping*): Hubert please! Please! Please! Half-wit!

The last phrase rings out sharply and brings instant stillness, but seems to please HUBERT.

HUBERT: 'it me Master Jack. Go on, 'it me, like your dad did. (*He offers his jaw and jigs again, hands behind his back.*) Like your dad did, like your dad did, like——

PENELOPE: Belt up, Hubert.

He stops. In the silence, MORGAN *goes and fetches* JACKO's *coat, carries it to him, helps him into it.*

Unbutton, Jacko. For God's sake unbutton . . .

JACKO, *head bent and silent, hastily buttons himself into his jacket.* MORGAN *pats his back and thus comforting him escorts him to the edge of the stage where exit* JACKO.

MORGAN (*to* HUBERT, *severely*): I shall report you to Madam. Do you understand?

PENELOPE: He doesn't care. Do you darling? Hubert's going to be the King.

MORGAN: Again?

PENELOPE: Who else?

MORGAN: You demean yourself.

PENELOPE: Who else could do it properly?

MORGAN: Penelope, ask yourself; what *is* it that *he* can do properly?

HUBERT: I can dig a ditch——!

PENELOPE *claps a hand delicately and quickly over his mouth, but he snatches it away.*

lay drain, mend fence, drive beast, lift load . . .

He ends gasping, glaring at MORGAN. PENELOPE *soothes him. Over his shoulder.*

PENELOPE: He can be King, properly.

MORGAN: Doesn't he remember what they did to him, last year?

PENELOPE: He had a good time last year. Didn't you Hubert?

HUBERT guffaws uneasily.

MORGAN: Then somebody should tell him – (*He speaks as one about to act.*)

She claps her hands on HUBERT's *ears, then removes one and points at* MORGAN.

PENELOPE: Hubert. You see that man there?

HUBERT: Yes my lady.

PENELOPE: Well he's a liar. Whatever that man tells you isn't true.

MORGAN: Jacko's right.

PENELOPE: Jacko isn't . . . Why, what does Jacko say?

MORGAN: That you are cruel.

PENELOPE: Are you a friend of Jacko's?

MORGAN: Yes within narrow limits.

PENELOPE: Well cut his buttons off; he's dying.

HUBERT gurgles, stamps.

PENELOPE: Come along. (*Leading him off.*) Hubert doesn't mind, Dr Morgan. Hubert hasn't got a mind.

The Forest thickens while:

Exit PENELOPE *and* HUBERT ¦Upstage *Left,* MORGAN *Right. Enter Downstage Right,* REVEREND *and* MRS TREADGOLD, CYNTHIA *and* GASTON. TREADGOLD *is lecturing eagerly, but the young couple immediately – though not hastily – sit and slumbrously embrace.*

TREADGOLD: The House itself is seventeenth century with additions, some of which I fear are of a recent date. However the façade remains intact. Now here's an interesting fact: There never was an Abbey here, yet Attis Abbey is its name – and thereby hangs a tale——

Turning, sees his audience oblivious. Crosses to MRS TREADGOLD.

Come Barbara.

MRS TREADGOLD (*looking up, surprised*): Oh.

TREADGOLD: I fear I am incommoding Miss Lazara's young guests.

   She looks past him, sees them, looks at him with anxious sympathy.

MRS TREADGOLD: Oh . . .

TREADGOLD: Come.

MRS TREADGOLD: Very well dear.

GASTON: Reverend Treadgold are you going? (*Good manners have called him from the private lovers' world. Not so* CYNTHIA.)

TREADGOLD: I think your interest in local history has run its course, Monsieur Dupont.

GASTON: Not at all. (*He slaps her caressing hand.*)

CYNTHIA: Ouch! Animal . . .

GASTON: Behave yourself.

CYNTHIA: I heard. There never was an Abbey here.

TREADGOLD: Ah . . . but there was!

CYNTHIA: You said there wasn't——

TREADGOLD: Well not in that sense——

CYNTHIA: What sense——?

GASTON: Be quiet: you are like a bluebottle.

CYNTHIA: Swat me.

GASTON: Would you like that?

CYNTHIA: Yes.

   They sink together again.

TREADGOLD: Come Barbara.

MRS TREADGOLD: I should like a cup of tea——

TREADGOLD: How thoughtless of me. Come. (*Wistful.*) I can tell them what I know another time . . .

MRS TREADGOLD: How selfish of me. Tell them now. (*Sits – pulling knitting from bag, calls to the lovers.*) My husband makes it very interesting.

GASTON (*briefly disengaging*): Yes he does.

TREADGOLD: How kind. (*To* MRS TREADGOLD) How kind. We first find mention made of Attis Abbey in the reign of Inulf. There was not then nor has been since a Church foundation here, but then as always just the Forest. The Forest itself then *is* the Abbey! (*His bombshell goes unnoticed. He falters*) 'Abbey' we may take to be a Christian synonym for 'Temple'. . . . Forgive me . . . For two thirds of my life I've had the privilege of the pulpit. (*Soberly*) I fear it's only too apparent.

GASTON: Not at all. Nobody would know.

TREADGOLD: How kind. How kind.

MRS TREADGOLD: 'Christian synonym for Temple.'

TREADGOLD: . . . for Temple. Attis Abbey thus becomes the Temple, or we might say Holy Place, of Attis. If we discount the Attis who was driven to a frenzy by his lover and castrated himself——

The lovers come unstuck.

MRS TREADGOLD: There dear, I knew you'd catch their interest.

CYNTHIA: What *kind* of frenzy?

TREADGOLD: Aha! The modern question, which the Ancients do not answer. They thought a frenzy self-explanatory. All they say is: She pursued and Attis ran and as he ran dropped blood upon the Forest floor, from which the scented violet was engendered. Before she caught him, Zeus in Pity . . . intervened: Transformed the mutilated man into a tree, 'A solitary fir, whose bark is like the hide of lions and whose needles sift the Western Wind, perpetually . . .'

They are all silent.

CYNTHIA: Stuffy old Zeus.

MRS TREADGOLD: One of his few creditable actions Lady Cynthia; it's a terrible old tale.

GASTON: It has the Mediterranean . . . strength.

TREADGOLD: Oh yes. That Attis never came much further north than Avignon. (*A little bow to* GASTON *gracefully acknowledged. Eagerly, to* CYNTHIA) The Attis we confront at dear old Attis Abbey is – I am convinced no less a personage than – well, than who?

CYNTHIA: Who?

TREADGOLD: Pan.

CYNTHIA: Pan.

TREADGOLD (*nodding*): Pan.

GASTON (*incredulous*): *Pan?*

TREADGOLD: The evidence is really quite strong——

GASTON: *Here?*

TREADGOLD: Our parish church for instance has some highly pagan corbel stones——

GASTON: But Pan – among all these – (*he is laughing*) wet woods?

TREADGOLD: Not by the very name of Pan. Jack-in-the-Green, an English variant.

MRS TREADGOLD: It is him we elect, tonight.

TREADGOLD: It is a very ancient ceremony.

> JACKO *in flight dashes across stage Left to Right, head back, going well, holding up his trousers from which the severed braces dangle.*

MRS TREADGOLD: Mr Cadence . . .

TREADGOLD: Junior.

> PENELOPE *in pursuit dashes across stage after* JACKO.

MRS TREADGOLD: Penelope Pelham.

CYNTHIA: Oh we've heard about her!

> JACKO *enters, Stage Right, stumbling, his trousers falling, revolving as he backs across the stage hopeful to have evaded the pursuit.* GASTON *watches with grave interest, the others with suppressed amusement. In the silence,* MRS TREADGOLD *lets escape a genteel titter from behind her hand.* JACKO *turns a shocked and frightened stare upon her. He goes. Instantly Stage Right enter* PENELOPE. *She carries a large pair of scissors. She stops, letting him go, panting, half laughing.* CYNTHIA *laughs sycophantically.*

PENELOPE: Who are you?

TREADGOLD: Lady Penelope Pelham, Lady Cynthia Dalrymple, Monsieur Dupont.

MRS TREADGOLD: I must follow him and apologize.

PENELOPE: Don't do that: you'll make him nasty.

She sits heavily on a garden bench, not looking at any of them, gloomy.

MRS TREADGOLD: Then I shall exercise Christian forbearance, Lady Penelope. There is no need for you to come, my dear. You did not laugh at him.

TREADGOLD: I laughed in spirit.

Exit TREADGOLDS. GASTON, *piqued that* PENELOPE's *self-absorption should exclude himself sets about its conquest, watched mistrustfully by* CYNTHIA.

GASTON: These seem to be very nice people.

PENELOPE: They are.

GASTON: He is an antiquarian.

PENELOPE: Yes.

GASTON: Is his information accurate?

PENELOPE: Dunno. Why, are you interested?

GASTON: No.

PENELOPE: Dupont?

GASTON: Dupont.

PENELOPE: Dupont Iron and Steel?

GASTON: My father. For the moment I am merely tinplate. The young man is very comical.

PENELOPE: Oh yes?

GASTON: . . . Forgive me.

PENELOPE: What for?

GASTON: I have the sensation of – Walking on eggs. Heavily.

PENELOPE: I feel nothing.

GASTON: They are hard-boiled perhaps.

CYNTHIA: Gaston!

GASTON: My bird?

He looms at her benevolently; she flutters.

CYNTHIA: I think we ought to go after him and apologize too.

GASTON: For what?

CYNTHIA: For laughing.

GASTON: I did not laugh.

CYNTHIA: But I did.

GASTON: Then you should apologize my bird.

Exit CYNTHIA, *dubious of them both.*

Adorable. I love her.

PENELOPE: You like your eggs very soft-boiled.

GASTON: Not boiled at all. Quite fresh.

PENELOPE: Is she quite fresh?

GASTON: Oh, perfectly.

PENELOPE: And will you boil her?

GASTON: Heaven forbid. Omelette au nature.

PENELOPE: Disgusting.

GASTON: Why?

PENELOPE: You're not even hungry.

GASTON: Heaven be thanked, I have never been hungry.

PENELOPE: You shouldn't eat then.

GASTON: Barbaric.

PENELOPE: You *love* her?

GASTON: As I understand it, utterly.

PENELOPE: Well, God help her.

GASTON: She is vital and trusting, and pretty and privileged. What does she need with God?

PENELOPE: Quite right. Go to it.

GASTON: Was that a mistake to let her go? She's difficult. You live difficult lives over here, do you not?

PENELOPE: I don't.

GASTON: No? She does. I should like to make it easier for her.

PENELOPE: You're a monster!

GASTON: You are wrong to say so. Nature and I are at one in this. I will confer a benefit on that little body.

PENELOPE: Are you sure?

GASTON: I swear it. And gently . . . Yes, it was a mistake. Excuse me.

Exit GASTON. *Immediately, enter* CYNTHIA *who has been*

in hiding. She walks up behind PENELOPE *and says with schoolgirl dignity:*

CYNTHIA: Please don't flirt with Gaston.

PENELOPE *sits up surprised, takes in the situation. Sympathetic.*

PENELOPE: You like him do you?

CYNTHIA: I'm dotty for him.

PENELOPE *considers her, hesitates, lies down again determinedly.*

PENELOPE: Then go and find him.

CYNTHIA: I'm frightened of him too.

PENELOPE: Then go home. Where d'you live?

CYNTHIA: Buckingham.

PENELOPE: I know a rhyme about Buckingham.

CYNTHIA: So do I. 'There once was a bishop of Buckingham——'

PENELOPE: I said I know it.

CYNTHIA: Sorry. (*Humbly*) All virgins are smutty.

PENELOPE: Did Gaston tell you that?

CYNTHIA: Yes.

PENELOPE: Go home.

But CYNTHIA *is sniffing where* GASTON *has sat, her expression tender.*

CYNTHIA: He uses scent.

PENELOPE: I noticed.

CYNTHIA: He's French.

PENELOPE: Get away!

CYNTHIA: We're in love.

PENELOPE: . . . Then go and find him.

CYNTHIA: What are you getting excited about?

PENELOPE: What?

CYNTHIA: Have you fallen for him?

PENELOPE (*very level*): Push off and find him, Cynthia.

CYNTHIA *wanders exit-wards.*

Don't worry; I'm not on the menu.

CYNTHIA: I don't know what to do.

PENELOPE: I've told you.

CYNTHIA: You say go home and then you say go after him.

PENELOPE: Ask someone else then. Ask Miss Lazara; she knows everything.

CYNTHIA: I wouldn't like to be like her. I'd like to be like you.

PENELOPE: I'd give it about a week.

CYNTHIA: Why do you pretend to be so tough? You're not so tough.

  No response.

  I think you're in love with Mr Cadence.

  A stunned silence. Then:

PENELOPE: Mr Cadence is *dead*! . . . Oh . . . (*Contemptuous*) Jacko.

CYNTHIA: Well, you were going to marry him.

PENELOPE: Convenience. I own the other half of the Forest.

  Her voice is dangerously flat, metallic, but CYNTHIA *rushes in, sly in her own conceit.*

CYNTHIA: Why didn't you marry the father then?

PENELOPE: He wanted me to marry Jacko. And he stank.

CYNTHIA: He what?

PENELOPE: Stank. He was dirty.

CYNTHIA: Ugh.

PENELOPE: He was something, was the father . . .

CYNTHIA: Ugh!

PENELOPE: I heard you. He used to breed bull-terriers for fighting.

CYNTHIA: Isn't that illegal?

PENELOPE: He used to kill his own cattle, with a pole-axe.

CYNTHIA: That *is* illegal!

PENELOPE: The old man now . . . yes . . . that might have been something.

CYNTHIA: Well how old was he?

PENELOPE: Seventy?

CYNTHIA: Bit long in the tooth.

PENELOPE (*deliberately coarse chuckle*): I bet he was a bit long everywhere. (*But throws her arm across her face and says with desperate sadness*) The father now . . . that really might have been . . . something.

CYNTHIA (*resentful, sharp, incredulous*): A dirty old man?

PENELOPE: . . . Virgins are smutty.

    CYNTHIA, *affronted, false-exits.*

Hey!

    CYNTHIA *half-unwillingly, returns.*

(*gently, chiding*) It's nothing wrong to be a virgin.

CYNTHIA: It's nothing anything.

PENELOPE (*considers this, accepts it*): Well try and notice, the first time. I didn't.

CYNTHIA: You're sentimental really. What's different about the first time?

    Exit CYNTHIA.

PENELOPE (*indifferently*): Lively little piece. (*She makes a slow tour of the stage. The circuit completed, she speaks as one who has made a difficult and unexpected realization.*) I wish, I wish I was a virgin . . . My word I'd notice! I'd notice the first time. (*Humbly corrects herself.*) I'd try. I always try. I tried the second time. And the third time, and the fourth and forty-fourth time. And I tried the five hundred and sixty-seventh time, last Sunday morning, with Samuel Simms in Billy Bowker's loft. Or was it Billy in Samuel's loft? The only difference I can notice is the number. I've got better at it certainly. Got good at it. Had some good teachers! And I think I may say I have a natural flair for it! I'm of an inventive turn of body I am! I am not a nice young woman! (*Quietly*) That makes no difference either. Practice makes practised; that's all that practice makes . . . The only time that's different is the first time because that's where you begin.

And presumably the last time because that's where you leave off. But you don't know which the last time is. It

might be something, if you did. Condemned men eat
hearty breakfasts. Yes, if you could know the last time – but
know – if you had taken in, digested and excreted *that* –
your appetites might put out branches, leaves and flowers,
your birds might sing, rivers run, and all your faculties,
notice! . . . My word, you'd need to know, though.

    Enter BRACKETS *holding hands, face audience, stop.*

And you can't know, can you?

BRACKET (*smiling calmly*): You can have a reasonable ex-
pectation, Lady Penelope.

PENELOPE: Is that enough?

MRS BRACKET (*smiling calmly*): It is if you will let it be, my
dear.

    PENELOPE, *baffled, withdraws from them and says to
audience:*

PENELOPE: It is for them; they're happily married. It's true –
the Reverend Treadgold happily married them. Twenty
years back. And they hold hands everywhere they go.

    She now 'freezes' Upstage Right. The BRACKETS *Down-
stage Left unclasp their hands.* MRS BRACKET *wipes her palm on
a handkerchief,* MR BRACKET *on his shirt. Then they clasp
hands again, firmly.*

BRACKET: I heard back from the lawyer.

MRS BRACKET: What did he say?

BRACKET: He asked if we'd thought about it long enough.

MRS BRACKET (*chuckles*): That's a good one.

BRACKET: If we'd talked it over thoroughly.

MRS BRACKET: Little does he know.

BRACKET: If we were sure divorce was what we wanted.

    A silence.

MRS BRACKET: What did you say?

BRACKET: I said – (*shamefaced*) no, I didn't think we were.

MRS BRACKET: Why did you say that?

BRACKET: I wasn't sure we were sure, Joy.

MRS BRACKET: Oh, Stirling!

BRACKET: Don't know why I said it really. Some sort of cowardice.

MRS BRACKET: No, you're not a coward.

BRACKET: What then?

MRS BRACKET: Lazy.

BRACKET: Lazy! This estate comprises four hundred acres of permanent grass, five hundred acres down to crops and a——

MRS BRACKET: You work hard at your work. But that's a kind of laziness.

BRACKET: Mm. Well that's a bit subtle for me I'm afraid.

MRS BRACKET: Don't let's quarrel, Stirling.

A silence.

BRACKET: It's going to be hot.

She doesn't hear him. He doesn't mind. Belatedly registering the noise of his voice she feels impelled to contribute to the conversation.

MRS BRACKET: It's going to be hot.

BRACKET: Aye. Well, as long as it keeps dry.

MRS BRACKET: Yes. I'm a regular sunflower for the heat; but I can't stand humidity.

BRACKET *grimaces swiftly. She hesitates, then:*

MRS BRACKET: Moisture.

BRACKET: I know what 'humidity' means, Joy. It's quite a common word.

MRS BRACKET: Well, of course you do.

BRACKET: Then why did you say 'moisture'?

MRS BRACKET: Oh Stirling, don't pick me up on every little thing.

BRACKET: Sorry.

MRS BRACKET: No, sorry.

A silence.

Not that it matters what the weather's like.

BRACKET: No.

MRS BRACKET: We don't notice it.

BRACKET: No.

MRS BRACKET: . . . Incapsulated.

BRACKET: I don't know about that. I know we used to get up early in the morning just to watch the sun rise!

MRS BRACKET: Through the river mist!

BRACKET: We used to know the phases of the moon!

MRS BRACKET: We used to notice when the wind moved round!

BRACKET: We used to go out in the rain!

MRS BRACKET: I *enjoyed* those early mornings!

BRACKET: Oh so did I . . .!

Reliving it they have been invigorated. Now the brightness fades from their faces. A drab sigh from BRACKET.

Well; the weather's still the same.

MRS BRACKET: We've altered.

BRACKET: I've not altered. I haven't, Joy. I've altered with you but I've not altered. I could get up early.

MRS BRACKET: So could I.

BRACKET: Not like that.

MRS BRACKET: I could.

BRACKET: With nothing on? (*Surprise makes him sound incredulous, even jeering.*)

MRS BRACKET: Yes. Don't be silly, dear. I couldn't look the same. No more could you. But I could feel the same. (*Friendly, but sly so that her tone too has the unintended note of jeering.*) I'm not so sure that you could.

BRACKET: Leave that to me.

MRS BRACKET: *Could* you?

BRACKET: I think so. – Not with *you.*

MRS BRACKET: Nor me with you dear.

A silence.

BRACKET: If we can't do it together, we ought to do it separately.

MRS BRACKET: Yes.

BRACKET: We *ought* to, Joy!

MRS BRACKET: Yes, Stirling, yes! It's——
BRACKET (*gently*): What?
MRS BRACKET: It's disgusting not to!
BRACKET: Poor Joy.

At some point in the above they have parted hands. Now they clasp again.

MRS BRACKET: Poor Stirling.

They face the audience exactly as at the beginning.

BRACKET: I'll write to the lawyer again tonight.
MRS BRACKET: No. I'll write.
BRACKET: Right. What does 'incapsulated' mean?
MRS BRACKET (*warningly*): Look out.

They wheel about still clasping hands as a procession enters. VIOLET *with* MORGAN, *the* TREADGOLDS, CYNTHIA *with* GASTON, HUBERT *with* CHAMPION, CHAMPION *in City clothes and carrying a letter.*

Good afternoon!

VIOLET: *Good* afternoon!
BRACKET: Hello there!
MRS BRACKET: Good afternoon!
VIOLET: Mrs Bracket; *Mr* Bracket. (*She takes each by the hand one after the other, carefully rejoining them.*) Though we have been here two days now I don't think everyone has met . . . I have had an important business communication from Mexico City and Mr Champion——

He raises hat.

has come all the way from London with it.

She has fetched up against the garden bench. MORGAN *indicates that she shall sit.*

MORGAN: You are over-excited.
VIOLET: And this is Dr Morgan, a mathematician and most valuable person. He teaches futility to my young men.
MORGAN: You will damage something presently.
VIOLET: Will everybody sit?

All the women but PENELOPE *sit, their men behind them.*

MORGAN *sits by* VIOLET, CHAMPION *and* HUBERT *stand behind her. Immediately she rearranges her little court to her better pleasure.*

Mr Treadgold, come and cast a blessing on me.

He joins CHAMPION.

Mrs Treadgold, you may knit. Monsieur Dupont, sit by me.

He does.

(*She sniffs at him vigorously.*) Delicious.

He kisses her hand, while:

Lady Cynthia, are you happy here?

CYNTHIA: Thank you yes, we *both* are.

VIOLET: Why, are there two of you?

CYNTHIA: When we can manage it.

GASTON: Cynthia!

VIOLET: No no Monsieur Dupont, when one is as charming as Lady Cynthia one should rub it in. Quite right, dear; be as vulgar as possible.

MORGAN: Now open the letter and calm yourself.

It seems she will obey, but her glance is arrested by PENELOPE *who is blowing down the front of her shirt.*

VIOLET: Have you lost something, Penelope?

PENELOPE: No everything seems to be here. (*As one explaining something esoteric.*) I'm sweating.

VIOLET: Small wonder; such an active life you lead. (*There is still a pair unseparated.*) Bracket, render your accounts.

BRACKET *with his bulky ledger moves behind her while she puts on spectacles. Peers at* MRS BRACKET. *Sharp:*

No sign of the stork, Mrs Bracket?

MRS BRACKET: No, just overeating. I've a terrible appetite!

BRACKET: She's a marvellous cook!

VIOLET (*taking ledger from him*): That will be the source of your serenity. A good cook, with a good appetite, must satisfy herself. Explain this.

BRACKET *leans over her shoulder to leaf the pages. Shrinking fastidiously from his hairy sleeve and its farmyard smells brings*

D

her within range of GASTON's *eau-de-Cologne. She leans towards him smiling brilliantly, while:*

BRACKET: Timber, Arable, Buildings, Livestock. Livestock subdivided, Milk, Meat, by-produce, subdivided, Hides, Hooves, Offal, Dung——

VIOLET: The figure! The figure!

    BRACKET *produces from the big ledger a tiny card at which she glances keenly.*

Satisfactory; I engage you for a further year.

BRACKET: Miss Lazara, I'm on a long-term contract!

VIOLET: I propose to honour it for another year.

MORGAN (*takes the letter, gives it to her*): Open it.

VIOLET (*takes it; hesitates; quietly*): You know that I would marry *you*, if your inclinations lay in that direction.

MORGAN: Safely said. You know that they do not.

    VIOLET *takes a picture postcard from the envelope while* MORGAN *looks politely elsewhere. On the back is something which makes her raise her eyebrows and smile. The picture makes her frown and clench it in her fist.*

Well?

VIOLET: A picture postcard. On the back, a figure. . . . on the front – a bullfight!

MORGAN: And is the figure good?

VIOLET: It's venomous. His obedience will cost me half a million.

MORGAN: Shall you buy it?

VIOLET: Yes. (*Frowns.*) I shall have to take the hotels with it. And I don't want them!

MORGAN: Then he had better stay and sell them too.

VIOLET: That will cost another million in his present mood.

MORGAN: I see that you are charmed.

VIOLET: Yes, wish me joy, my friend.

MORGAN: Joy?

VIOLET: Joy. I am charmed.

HUBERT: Hello Young Master Jack.

Enter JACKO *on squeaking boots. He stops short as* VIOLET *turns to face him.*

VIOLET: Pat on another man's cue. How is it he distracts me?

MORGAN: It's complicated.

   JACKO *starts forward.*

VIOLET: It's his boots!

JACKO: Miss Lazara——

VIOLET: Take them off!

   He kneels obediently.

MRS TREADGOLD: Oh poor young man . . .

VIOLET: Well, leave them.

JACKO: No that's all right . . .

VIOLET: Leave them, leave them, what d'you want?

JACKO: No really I don't mind. They do – (*tugging off one boot*) – squeak.

VIOLET: *Leave* them!

   He rises. It seems he will go, but——

PENELOPE: Go away you fool.

JACKO: It's about tonight Miss Lazara. You should stop it.

VIOLET: What happens tonight?

BRACKET (*deprecating*): Just local high jinks.

   Unwittingly he has snubbed her. The others compound the offence by arguing among themselves, excluding her.

CYNTHIA: High jinks?

PENELOPE: – We relax a bit that's all.

GASTON: – Then let it not by any means be stopped!

MRS TREADGOLD: – It *has* got out of hand on one or two occasions . . .

MRS BRACKET: – It got out of hand last year.

CYNTHIA: – Out of hand?

PENELOPE (*contemptuous*): – There was an accident.

MRS TREADGOLD: – It was no accident.

BRACKET (*correcting them all*): – Last year, Miss Lazara wasn't here.

TREADGOLD: – It's a very old *custom*!

PENELOPE: – Hundreds of years!

TREADGOLD: – The ceremony itself is harmless surely?

MRS TREADGOLD: – But Cedric the Labourers——

MRS BRACKET: – Yes. It's the Labourers.

JACKO: – the Labourers——

VIOLET: What heaps of nothing! (*She silences them.*) It is a country custom kept alive by Townies. The labourers will be in Monmouth at the Cinema. It's for the house-servants. Out-of-work waiters, unemployables, ex-Navy men! Don't play Old English here. Your father's father bought this place with money made from railway shares.

CHAMPION: Money from railway shares . . . Ah me, the Pageant of History.

All are glad to smile.

VIOLET: I appeal to you. Could anything look less Squire-archal?

CHAMPION: No. A thorough-going City man is Mr Cadence.

VIOLET: Stuff. The way he wears a City suit's the only rustic thing about him.

All are amused. Even HUBERT, *aware that* JACKO *is in some way being baited, guffaws and slaps his knee.*

Remember, Hubert, if a City man can't wear a City suit he can't do anything. It is his only function.

CHAMPION: I protest!

VIOLET (*to* JACKO): You are excused.

The others watch amused as JACKO *goes, peg-legged and warily. His one boot squeaks violently.*

MORGAN (*kindly impatience*): Put them *both* on Jacko.

PENELOPE: Take them both off.

He looks from one to the other. Finds his own solution. Exit hopping. All but MRS TREADGOLD *laugh, starting individually, achieving the ritual harsh barking* HA HA HA HA HA HA HA! *and ending individually again.*

MRS TREADGOLD (*to* CYNTHIA): Why do you laugh at him?

VIOLET: Lady Cynthia is the mirror of society. She laughs because it is proper. Till tonight then!

ALL: Till tonight!

On this they rise and disperse but are arrested by:

VIOLET (*to* MORGAN, *to be overheard*): Mrs Treadgold thinks me cruel. Am I?

MORGAN: Not more than average.

VIOLET: Ah yes, most people are cruel. Are they not?

MORGAN: Not specially.

MRS TREADGOLD: I find them so.

MORGAN: When we say a person is *specially* cruel we *mean*; more cruel than most. 'Most people' can't be 'specially' anything. I think you mean that Jacko's specially sensitive to cruelty.

MRS BRACKET: Or else most people are specially cruel to Jacko.

MORGAN: If they are, it will be because he's specially sensitive.

MRS TREADGOLD (*diffident*): Well isn't that, specially cruel?

Murmur of surprised, amused admiration for her, in which VIOLET *joins, for* MORGAN'*s displeasure.*

MORGAN: No no. Take ten as a constant quantity of cruelty——

PENELOPE (*flat*): You can't.

MORGAN: Can't what?

PENELOPE: Take ten. It can't be measured.

MORGAN: Cruelty is an impulse in a body. Bodies are made of matter. Matter can be measured. In principle, everything is measurable.

VIOLET: Hm. 'Till tonight then!

The sunlight fades swiftly. Exit all but HUBERT, CHAMPION, MORGAN *and* VIOLET.

My tame philosopher. How *is* my tame philosopher?

MORGAN: Tame, as you insist. Do you flatter yourself that you would relish a wild one?

Exit VIOLET *and* MORGAN. CHAMPION *and* HUBERT *are left, as the light darkens into night. At length,* CHAMPION *tips his hat and is going.*

HUBERT: Hey!

CHAMPION: Yes?

HUBERT: Hey.

CHAMPION: At your disposal.

HUBERT: Are you her man?

CHAMPION: I am Miss Lazara's Director of Accounts.

HUBERT: How much has she got then?

CHAMPION: Our assets in round figures are, twenty-five millions of real estate, twelve-and-a-half millions gilt-edged stock, nineteen millions industrials, nine millions in municipal bonds, mostly South American, and then we have controlling interests in Trading Trusts with Active Assets of say thirty millions and a half.

HUBERT: That's a hundred and one millions. (*Advancing.*) How did she come by it?

CHAMPION: She had it from her father.

HUBERT: How did he?

CHAMPION: By his operations in the City.

HUBERT: Oh. Can't be fairly come by. I get eight pounds a week for cutting hedges.

CHAMPION: The activities are hardly comparable.

HUBERT: I reckon I could learn to wear that suit quicker'n you could learn to cut a hedge.

CHAMPION: It's not as easy as it looks. Consider Mr Cadence.

HUBERT: Him!

Exit both, as moonlight crosses stage, revealing JACKO, *who looks after them.*

JACKO: Is it thought because I am a fool I am too much a fool to feel it?

Noises off. Enter SERVANTS, *two* LABOURERS, *and* GRIEVES, *Upstage obscured by foliage, carrying paper wands. They progress in the same direction as the moonlight, desultory, as men half on duty, fooling, laughing, talking as they enter, then:*

1ST SERVANT: 'Evening, Mr Cadence!

A moment's silence, then:

2ND SERVANT: That *you*, Mr Cadence?

3RD SERVANT (*half whisper, to others*): Who's that?

2ND SERVANT: That's Mr Cadence, that is.

1ST SERVANT: Mr Cadence's son.

2ND SERVANT: Mr Cadence that was, that is.

1ST SERVANT: Him with the fists.

2ND SERVANT: You're not like that, are you Mr Cadence?

JACKO (*peering Upstage*): Is that you, Foley?

His voice produces another momentary silence, then:

GRIEVES (*flatly*): No, Foley's gone.

OLD LABOURER: 'Ow be on, Master Jack?

Whoops, jeers.

YOUNG LABOURER (*caricatured West Country*): 'Evenin' Zquoire!

YOUNG LABOURER is shoved from behind. Quarrelsome and jocular, all but JACKO exit. The moonlight still working.

JACKO: It seems that Nature's made me inside out and all my active outer parts like fists and teeth are cramped in here (*his stomach*); and all that uncouth stuff which should be left in darkness, is exhibited, in me.

Enter TREADGOLD with CYNTHIA, MRS TREADGOLD, with GASTON, in changed clothes, TREADGOLD carrying particularly elaborated versions of the paper wands.

TREADGOLD: The King of Folly, the Germanic Walber, here called Jack-in-the-Green, the Lord of License. You will find a very lively likeness of him underneath my pulpit.

CYNTHIA: Underneath?

TREADGOLD: The underside, you'll need a torch; he's up to no good I'm afraid.

CYNTHIA (*delighted*): And we're going to elect him?

TREADGOLD: Strictly speaking we elect the King of Folly who is human. We invoke Jack-in-the-Green who is a god.

GASTON: How?

TREADGOLD: By sacrifice. (*Distributes wands.*) A hen for Lady Cynthia, a cow for you, Monsieur Dupont. Will you have this, my dear?

MRS TREADGOLD: No.

GASTON: What is that?

TREADGOLD: Formalized past recognition, but I fear it may have been a man.

CYNTHIA: But when we've elected him what do we *do*?

TREADGOLD: In ancient days his rule was absolute and everyone partook in it. There's some suspicion that period of Folly was atoned for with the poor man's blood. (*Cheerful.*) But we don't know that for certain, no. Nowadays, a week of – nothing really – and a purely token punishment.

GASTON: Aha. We dispense with the folly and retain the punishment. Rule Britannia.

TREADGOLD: Oho. A Gallic thrust! What chance should we stand in the Common Market! This way! This way! It's deeper in the Forest!

Exit, following the SERVANTS. *The Forest thickens. Enter* VIOLET *agitated,* MORGAN *soothing, both in changed clothes.*

VIOLET: Half a million to buy them and another million to sell them.

MORGAN: Is it too much?

VIOLET: It's a little spirited!

MORGAN: You like a man with spirit.

VIOLET: I also like obedience!

MORGAN: It's just right then.

VIOLET: He has calculated!

MORGAN: Yes, but perfectly.

VIOLET: He has won!

MORGAN: No no.

VIOLET: Then have *I* won? . . . Morgan, make me see that.

MORGAN: I can't; you haven't; you mustn't.

VIOLET: No . . . You are very wise. And very kind. Very wise and kind . . . It must be a balance . . .

MORGAN: Yes.

VIOLET: *No* dammit! He's 'mated' me – with my own money!

MORGAN: Very well then, order him to stay in Mexico until he's sold them at a profit.

VIOLET: . . . I don't want him in Mexico!

MORGAN: Order him to be celibate until he's sold them at a profit.

VIOLET: His obedience wouldn't cover that . . .

MORGAN: No. Obedience, doesn't.

She whirls; he spreads his hands apologetically as one who can do no other.

VIOLET: Oh correct! Correct! A little glib perhaps but sub-humanly correct!

MORGAN: I'll leave you now, Violet.

VIOLET (*calls after him*): No. Not kind. Cold.

He stops.

Absolute zero!

MORGAN: Yes, I'll leave you.

VIOLET: You are a gap in the ranks of humanity!

He stops, returns.

Help me!

MORGAN: I can't.

JACKO: Miss Lazara——

They see him together.

VIOLET: No . . .!

JACKO: Last year they tarred and feathered Hubert and hung him in a tree.

VIOLET: Who did?

MORGAN: Come.

VIOLET: No. Who did?

JACKO: The workers.

VIOLET: The workers do nothing. Who did?

JACKO: Miss Lazara you *exaggerate* my father!

VIOLET: Exaggerate? He was the merest animal.

JACKO: Yes but you have this sense of guilt!

VIOLET: – of——?

JACKO: Guilt.

VIOLET: – of——?

MORGAN: Jacko!

VIOLET: Guilt! (*To* MORGAN, *terribly quiet.*) You have talked about me. (*To* JACKO. *Terribly contemptuous.*) Go back to the house and work. (*To* MORGAN.) You have talked about me; with this – idiot. (*Passing him, she seizes the wand and exits.*)

MORGAN: You've ruined yourself. Come back to the house.

> *Exit* MORGAN *opposite. The foliage thickens again, becoming oppressive, smothering the moonlight. Enter* SERVANTS *and* LABOURERS. *They carry four white pillars which they set up in a square, and a small white pedestal which they place between the pillars.*

GRIEVES: What I want to know is this: are we here on duty, or are we here for fun?

> *A scornful grumbling rises from* SERVANTS, *collective and indecipherable in content though clear in tone.*

2ND SERVANT (*examining his wand distastefully*): Lot of thick-wit nonsense.

OLD LABOURER: No 't'isn't——

YOUNG LABOURER: Hey Dad——

OLD LABOURER: Yes——?

YOUNG LABOURER: Shurrup.

> OLD LABOURER *quelled.* YOUNG LABOURER *looks at* GRIEVES.

GRIEVES: Because what I want to know is this: Are we being paid for this or are we not?

> PENELOPE *enters Upstage among foliage.*

PENELOPE (*contemptuously*): Why don't you relax?

SERVANTS *and* LABOURERS *turn heavily to face her.*

GRIEVES: Can't afford to on eight quid a week, Miss.

PENELOPE: You couldn't relax on eight quid an hour.

GRIEVES: I'll try Miss, if you'll pay me that.

PENELOPE: Not likely.

GRIEVES: Easy said then, Miss.

JACKO (*sycophantic eagerness*): Jolly good!

SERVANTS *and* LABOURERS *turn heavily back.*

GRIEVES: What's that, sir?

JACKO: . . . Jolly good.

GRIEVES: You're on *our* side are you sir?

JACKO (*eager*): I am about this thing tonight. It *is* a lot of nonsense.

He backs off as they advance upon him.

2ND SERVANT: What do *you* get Mr Cadence?

1ST SERVANT: Aye, what's the rate, Mr Cadence?

3RD SERVANT: Tell us Mr Cadence, what d'you get?

PENELOPE: Tell them, Jacko!

JACKO: A thousand a quarter.

They stop.

GRIEVES: Eighty pounds a week.

2ND SERVANT: *You* get eighty pounds a week?

JACKO: We all do . . .

They swing about again and leave him, exclaiming softly, deeply angered.

GRIEVES: *He's* on *our* side.

JACKO: Look!

They turn in silence, expecting orders.

Look . . . you seem a decent lot of blokes.

At once they turn about again and leave him finally, with exclamations of distaste and dismissal.

As they move, enter REVEREND TREADGOLD *and his party. The two parties cross, and as they do so:*

TREADGOLD (*sing-song, but meticulously individual*): Good evening, Good evening, Good evening, Good evening

Sam. Good evening . . . (*He has missed* YOUNG LABOURER.)
  TREADGOLD *fetches up Centre Stage.*

YOUNG LABOURER: Good evening.

TREADGOLD: Good evening! Well! Where is the hero of the hour?

  HUBERT *enters and stands somewhat shyly before the 'Temple'.* JACKO *starts towards him.*

JACKO: Hubert——!

  But SERVANTS *and* LABOURERS *are also moving towards him.*

2ND SERVANT: Here he is!

1ST SERVANT: Here's Einstein!

3RD SERVANT: Hello Gormless!

GRIEVES: What's he supposed to be?

3RD SERVANT: The Queen of the May!

LABOURER: Got your best knickers on, Hubert?

  They form a wall of backs between HUBERT *and* JACKO.

JACKO: Hubert——!

1ST SERVANT: Seen any nice girls lately, Hubert?

2ND SERVANT: How's your sister?

3RD SERVANT: How's your mother?

2ND SERVANT: How's your pig?

HUBERT: Hey!

  They fall silent.

  Hey . . .

  They crowd round him expectantly, listening. He addresses himself to YOUNG LABOURER. *We hear the mumbling of his rural brogue; he is telling a joke. At the climax, all but the* YOUNG LABOURER *fly apart, with delighted disgust.*
  (*To* YOUNG LABOURER, *following up what he considers to have been a social success.*) I will! I will! Tonight!

  YOUNG LABOURER *pushes him violently. He staggers back, is pushed forward by another, and back up and down an impromptu running gauntlet, with whoops and laughter.*

TREADGOLD: Men! Men! Men!

He flutters ineffectually. JACKO *intervenes and is himself caught up in the gauntlet for a moment, shuttling back and forth reciprocal with* HUBERT.

TREADGOLD: Men! Men!

Enter MR *and* MRS BRACKET.

BRACKET: That's enough!

Instant stillness.

BRACKET: Good evening Mr Cadence.

JACKO (*crossing, head bowed*): I'm sorry. Thank you.

PENELOPE: Oh you're painful!

GRIEVES (*politely*): Are we here on duty then, sir?

BRACKET: You're here because it's an ancient custom which Miss Lazara and her guests would like to see. It's also one of the dying traditions of your country which you're privileged to help keep alive. If you can't see that I'm sorry for you.

GRIEVES: Yes sir. (*Exactly as before.*) Are we here on duty?

BRACKET: All right, Grieves, you're on duty.

GRIEVES: Thank you, sir.

CYNTHIA: I like Grieves. Are you jealous?

GASTON: Passionately. (*Then gravely.*) Passionately.

OLD LABOURER: 'Tis a close old night then.

MR *and* MRS BRACKET *are holding hands Front Stage Right.*

MRS BRACKET: You're doing it again.

BRACKET: What?

MRS BRACKET: Making that clicking noise with your teeth.

BRACKET: Sorry. (*Unclasps hand and adjusts dentures.*) I'll get a set made by a private dentist.

Having done it he must wipe his hand; she takes the opportunity to do the same.

MRS BRACKET: Using what for money?

BRACKET: No it's a foul noise, that clicking with your teeth. (*Clasps hands again.*) You do it too.

HUBERT: Hey!

All swing to face him.

What's ten and nine and eight and twelve and – and seventy-two and (*excited*) a hundred and ninety take away three?

They regard him stonily.

JACKO: About four hundred, Hubert.

HUBERT: No . . .

A melody is heard to be emanating from SERVANTS *and* LABOURERS. *It grows louder.*

SERVANTS *and* LABOURERS: 'Why are we waiting, why-y are we waiting, why are we wai-ai-ting, why oh why? Why are we——'

BRACKET *turns round. Under his gaze the song dies reluctantly away, the bolder holding out longer.* BRACKET *turns back. Silence.*

2ND SERVANT (*softly and bitterly*): . . . Eighty quid a week . . .

Thus all are looking at JACKO, *and* VIOLET *makes her entrance unseen. She is still angry.*

VIOLET: Come along then Mr Treadgold.

TREADGOLD: Oh. Oh. Shall we commence?

VIOLET: It's five to midnight. We've not had supper.

TREADGOLD: Five to! Well then.

He mounts the pedestal. He stands still. The others show a mild interest except for VIOLET *who is occupied by her own thoughts. Suddenly* TREADGOLD *begins, not rhetorically, but seriously, as a man who has thought about it:*

Jack in y greene leaves myld

Jack in y greene woodland wyld

Jack in y grete tronkes pyld——

Com to us, who byn begyld!

VIOLET: Is Doctor Morgan here?

JACKO: Er – no——

VIOLET: I told you to go to the house and work!

TREADGOLD *coughs.*

Yes, yes.

TREADGOLD (*with more feeling now, and the others listen, even* VIOLET):
Banyshed be we fro blys
Tho our faulte nothyng is,
By crafte and pretence
For Adam hys offens!
Longe tyme we bounden be,
Comen thou and mak us fre,
Greefe our herte has,
How come we to thys pas?

    VIOLET *twitches her wand impatiently. The sudden movement in the stillness draws all eyes to her.*

Perhaps I should abbreviate?

PENELOPE: No!

    JACKO *engages* HUBERT *in mimed conversation, urgent.*

VIOLET: As you wish, Mr Treadgold . . . Yes. A short service by all means.

TREADGOLD (*descending*): Lady Cynthia, Monsieur Dupont—— (*He takes their wands from them.*) Pennies ready everybody! (*He sticks the wands, with his own, into the ground before the pedestal, saying quietly:*)
Black hen giving white eggs, black cow giving white milk, and this . . .

    The rest are watching him closely and draw a little towards him as he remounts and louder, clearer, with a marked rhythmic beat:
By-cause of thee the cock doth sprynge
By-cause of thee his mate doth synge
By thee she syngs her fill
By thee he hath his wyl!
Never thou did we forsake
But we did thee al-onely make.
Now pence to thee we gyf.
And thinges three that lyf!
(*breathless*) Pence! Pence!

At the appropriate moment all throw coins, in the spirit of the thing now, as TREADGOLD *goes straight on.*

Without our lyking liven we
Come thou and our greene master be
Not we did thee forsake
See we thy livry take . . . (*breathless*)
Livery take!

All raise wands. Begin to join in.

Banyshed be we fro blys,
Tho our faulte nothyng is,
Greefe our herte has!

In unison:

How com we to thys pas?

In unison:

Now cock shall sprynge
And hen shall synge
And green Jack is our King!
His name, his name!

PENELOPE: What?

TREADGOLD: His name!

PENELOPE: Hubert!

At this point whispered conversation between HUBERT *and* JACKO *becomes animated,* JACKO *gesturing.*

BRACKET ⎫
CYNTHIA ⎬ Hubert!
GASTON ⎪
1ST SERVANT ⎭

ALL: Hubert!

HUBERT (*stepping forward towards* SERVANTS): No!

Silence abruptly. Sly, as one who knows a thing or two:

Oh no. No. Hubert knows.

YOUNG LABOURER *takes a step forward. Instantly* HUBERT's *foolish grin is replaced by a glare of determination and he crouches.*

Gerr!

YOUNG LABOURER *stops.*

Hubert knows now. Hubert knows now what you done.

OLD LABOURER: T'weren't this lot Hubert, that lot's gone.

HUBERT: Doan' you worry 'bout that my boy . . .

MRS BRACKET: But Hubert, you can't think that Miss Lazara would allow anything like that.

HUBERT: Hubert knows . . .

They are nonplussed.

(*very sly.*) 'T'was Master Jack as told me . . .

All look at JACKO.

PENELOPE: Then Jacko!

GASTON: Jacko!

TREADGOLD: Jacko?

MUSIC *rising.*

BRACKET: Come on Jacko!

MRS BRACKET: Have a go, do, Mr Cadence!

PENELOPE: Jacko!

MUSIC *rising.*

CYNTHIA
HUBERT
YOUNG LABOURER } (*raggedly*): Jacko!
BRACKET

MUSIC *full blast.*

SERVANTS *and* LABOURERS: Jacko!

JACKO: Miss Lazara!

VIOLET: Jacko!

JACKO *backs up towards the Temple and* TREADGOLD, *but with a rush the* SERVANTS *and* LABOURERS *are on him, bowl him over, shouting like schoolboys, while* GASTON *and* BRACKET *agitate equivocally on the edge of the scrum. All lurch away dragging items of clothing.* JACKO *is left, seemingly naked. He rises. They rush back at him laughing – and festoon him with garlands. They break away but in a close circle so that he is still obscured, and laugh:* HA HA HA HA HA HA HA! *While:*

E

HUBERT (*beside himself, hopping as before*): 'It me, Master Jack! 'It me, Master Jack! 'It me, Master Jack——!

 Suddenly JACKO *rushes at him. A moment of confusion and all scatter, dragging* HUBERT *backwards with them. Blood is streaming down his face. With whoops, laughter, exclamations of shock or fear all exit in a twinkling.* JACKO *puts his face in his hands and sobs. The* MUSIC *starts. At the same time another area of light is made behind the foliage Upstage.* A FIGURE *stands in it.*

 This is JACK. JACKO *becomes aware of him, takes his face from his hands, turns, sees him, starts.* JACK *makes an apologetic gesture, then steps towards him.* JACKO *flees but* JACK *raises a hand. There is a drum-thump and cymbal crash like that of a circus clown's prat-fall, and* JACKO *is felled.* JACKO *backs away from* JACK *in the widest possible arc and runs and the same thing happens, then a third time:*

 JACK *raises a hand.*

 JACKO *prat-falls.*

JACK: You'll hurt yourself.

 He advances, JACKO *shuffles backwards on his bottom, staring. Tactfully,* JACK *stops and turns away. His eye lights on the litter of wands and garlands. He picks one up.*

I have *never* seen it done worse. If it weren't for that idiot priest, who does at any rate know the words, I doubt if I'd be here at all!

 JACKO *stares in silence.* JACK *squats on the pedestal.*

How d'you feel?

 JACKO *stares.*

Nerves all of a jangle are they?

 JACKO *stares.*

Like sea-sick? Mm . . . have an apple. Or an orange. Or a pear.

 An apple, an orange, a pear fall from the trees above. JACKO *stares up wildly.*

(*looking up, he calls*) Let's have some music!

INSECT MUSIC.

JACK: . . . Cat got your tongue?

    JACKO *half-rises to flee; very slowly* JACK's *hand gestures him irresistibly down again.*

I shan't harm you. Matter of fact I couldn't. Not to say harm. Not considering the harm you've done yourself.

    JACKO *looks at him.*

You understood that! You understood immediately. Oh you're a wise one. I said that to myself, oh, years ago. 'This one's going to be a wise one' I said. I admire human beings – well—— yes, yes, I do, I admire them.

    JACKO *passes an arm across his brow, bewildered.*

Are you hot? You're hot. It is hot here.

    Snow falls.

. . . Snow.

    JACKO *puts out a finger, takes a flake, puts it on his tongue. He starts half to his feet but is thrown down by a gesture from* JACK.

Now don't! . . . I've waited a long time for you . . . I shan't harm you . . . Why should *I* harm anyone? (*He approaches the three 'totems'. He takes a great knife from its sheath. It must be like a razor, for it whips the heads off the third very neatly. He puts away the knife. He picks up the 'totem'.*) . . . My word, they're economical. . . . (*Shows it to* JACKO.) Paper. What do they expect for that?

CURTAIN

ACT TWO

The stage is as for end Act One, except that the temple, the snow, and all debris have gone, and the green gloom is transfixed by sloping pillars of fiery white sunshine. MORGAN *stands centre.*

MORGAN: Jacko!
    Enter BRACKETS.
No sign of him in the North Ride, Mr Bracket.
MRS BRACKET: No sign of him in the South Ride either.
    Enter TREADGOLDS.
TREADGOLD: No sign of him in the East Ride, I'm afraid.
    Enter PENELOPE *followed by* HUBERT. *All look to her enquiringly.*
PENELOPE: Hey, someone's killed my dog!
MRS BRACKET: What?
PENELOPE: Yes.
TREADGOLD: Little Queenie?
BRACKET: Your little black lurcher?
MRS TREADGOLD: Oh no!
MORGAN (*sceptical*): What d'you mean, 'killed'?
PENELOPE: You know, like – dead.
BRACKET (*constabular*): Poison?
HUBERT: Knife.
BRACKET: Knife! (*Stares hard at* HUBERT.)
HUBERT: I found her. T'weren't *me*.
    They look at one another, startled.
    MORGAN *calls.*
MORGAN: Jacko!

PENELOPE: Jacko? Can't kill a cockerel. He can't – he'd starve to death on a poultry farm.

Enter GASTON *and* CYNTHIA.

GASTON: We found this fruit, Bracket.

Hands pear to BRACKET, *retains orange.*

BRACKET: He's all right Dr Morgan. He must have been into the house for these.

Enter CHAMPION.

CHAMPION: Good morning. Miss Lazara is rising. She has asked for Mr Cadence.

MRS BRACKET: We can't find him.

CHAMPION: It's rather awkward. We return to Town.

PENELOPE: That should fetch him. (*Calls.*) Jacko, Miss Lazara wants you! You're going back to Town.

Silence.

'I'll stay out in the woods I will, and then they'll be sorry.'

MORGAN: He is more serious, less secure, than you have any comprehension of.

MRS TREADGOLD: I think we pressed him, very hard you know.

MORGAN: By all accounts, yes.

PENELOPE: He doesn't matter! I don't mind . . .

MRS BRACKET: I say, this is a very good pear!

MORGAN *gives her his coldest attention; she looks guilty. Loud sucking noises from* CYNTHIA. *All look towards her. She is eating the orange with simian greed. She looks up to encounter* MORGAN'S *refrigerating eyebeam, 'freezes' guiltily.*

MORGAN: Considering the circumstances, no one seems to mind much.

They rise.

TREADGOLD (*plaintive*): It's the weather, one can't mind anything.

MORGAN: I mind!

Exit TREADGOLDS.

PENELOPE: Mind for me will you?

MORGAN: Seemingly.

Exit PENELOPE *and* HUBERT *one way,* MORGAN *following* TREADGOLDS, GASTON *hauls* CYNTHIA *to her feet.*

CYNTHIA: Oh why don't they fetch the police?

GASTON: No no . . .

CYNTHIA: My bra's broken.

GASTON: Mm hm . . . ?

Exit GASTON *and* CYNTHIA *after* MORGAN. BRACKET *rising,* MRS BRACKET *being linked must follow.*

BRACKET: Come on, back towards the House.

On which foliage flies, partially revealing House. Also JACK *and* JACKO *prone and dressed identically. Exit* BRACKETS *after others.*

JACK: Don't you want to be happy?

JACKO: Yes.

JACK: I mean, just innocently happy?

JACKO: Oh God yes.

JACK: Do take these off (JACKO's *spectacles*).

JACKO: I need them.

JACK: No you don't.

JACKO: I need them for close work.

JACK: No close work here. (*Takes them. Goes on.*) Well if that's what you want——?

JACKO: But——

JACK: Then do what you want.

JACKO: But——

JACK: You don't want to hurt anybody, do you?

JACKO: Sometimes.

JACK (*pauses, cautiously, then*): That's because your nature's been distorted.

JACKO: I do feel distorted.

JACK: 'T isn't your fault.

JACKO: Isn't it?

JACK: You had an unhappy childhood.

JACKO *twists up to look at him, sharply.*

JACKO: That's not very original.

JACK: You're so *sharp*! Well if you want the truth – It *is* your fault.

JACKO (*settling back*): I knew it was.

JACK: What I mean – you had to save yourself.

JACKO: Yes.

JACK: Any way you could.

JACKO: I suppose so.

JACK: I'll teach you how to spend yourself.

>JACKO *thinks, sighs hopelessly, rolling his head.*

I'll teach you. I am a god. I am a very, great, god.

>JACKO *looks up into the divine countenance and is comforted.*

Hey, d'you want a giggle?

>JACKO *sits back as one ready to appreciate the antics of an amusing companion. From behind him* JACK *lugs the carcass of a black dog.* JACKO *starts back on his haunches. With the triumphant air of a conjurer* JACK *spins it about. Its underbelly gapes open and a mess of glistening entrails hangs out. The bees roar suddenly.* JACKO *recoils galvanically, pointing, horrified.*

JACKO: What's that?

JACK: A dog.

JACKO: Who *did* it?

JACK (*puzzled*): I did.

JACKO: Why?

JACK (*utterly at sea*): 'Why'?

JACKO (*desperate*): What *for*?

JACK: 'For'?

>JACKO *looks at* JACK's *blankly innocent face and flies.* JACK *casts the carcass from him.*

Stop!

>JACKO *is arrested.*

Now listen. If you want, you can go. You can go. And tell yourself, you 'met an "incubus", a "goblin", "boggart", "sprite", "demon", "devil", "imp", "elf", "troll", "hallucination".' Ha! You 'were "bewitched", "possessed",

"enchanted", "had a nervous breakdown" ' . . . In the
Forest. If you want. But you'll have had your one chance –
Jacko! Isn't that the truth? . . . However, if you want . . .
(*He turns away on this, seemingly indifferent.*)

JACKO *finds that he can move and at once* JACK *turns and
yells, malignant and pathetic.*

Go on! Back to your sadness and your resignation and
reduction, and your unlived life – that's beginning to stink
on you d'you know that? Go on! Back to your avoided
days. Your abstract hours, your millions of disembodied
minutes! And your heavy dreams – that are destroying
you d'you know that?

(*beseeching*) Or stay, and let me help you . . . There is a
place for you in Nature.

JACKO *looks at him.*

How could there not be? You have no other place. Oh
damn, she's coming. (*He has not looked off.*)

JACKO: Who?

JACK: Penelope.

JACKO *looks off startled, can't see her, looks startled back.*

She's coming. Let me help! And if I don't may lightning
strike me. I'll be here but she won't see me. Let me help.
Take courage from me, I have it. Take ease, it's mine. Take
dignity. Here I am. There she is. She won't see me.

JACKO: Why not?

JACK: She can't.

JACKO: Why not?

JACK: She won't. Here she is.

They see her.

(*he grips* JACKO's *arm*): Take a light heart! (*Almost desperate.*)
Borrow it, borrow! And *trust* me!

And on that word he seizes JACKO's *hand and thrusts his
knife into it and* PENELOPE *enters.*

PENELOPE: Jacko! . . . (*Seeing the dog.*) What's that?

JACK (*beside* JACKO): Your dog.

PENELOPE: Who *did* it?

JACK: I did.

PENELOPE (*to* JACKO): *You* did?

    JACK *grips him by the arm.*

JACKO (*faintly*): I did.

JACK: Splendid!

PENELOPE: What?

JACKO (*more strongly*): I did.

PENELOPE: *Why?*

JACKO (*again gripped by* JACK): 'Why'?

PENELOPE: What for?

JACKO (*rather arrogantly*): 'For'?

JACK: She's all yours darling, take her away!

PENELOPE (*bewildered*): What?

JACKO (*indicating carcass*): I've finished with her.

JACK: You're a natural!

    And now JACKO *actually shakes off* JACK's *grip as an impediment.*

PENELOPE (*trying for anger*): Did you call me 'darling'?

JACKO: Yes.

PENELOPE (*rises dangerously from the carcass, but recoils*): There's blood on your face!

JACK: There was blood in the dog——

JACKO:——darling.

    PENELOPE *now backs away round* JACKO *in the widest arc, exactly as did* JACKO *when he first saw* JACK. JACK *sits apart to watch the fun.*

PENELOPE: . . . You're off your head.

JACKO: No I'm not.

PENELOPE: . . . You look a proper nit.

JACKO: No I don't.

    PENELOPE's *breath comes short. She has a brilliant idea.*

PENELOPE: Miss Lazara wants you.

JACK (*to* JACKO): Who?

PENELOPE: Miss Lazara!

JACKO: Don't know the lady. Have an apple. Have an orange——

    JACK *rises, alarmed, but his protégé has the bit between his teeth and he must cause the fruit to fall.*

—Have a melon.

    PENELOPE *jumps as it falls with a crash, stares wildly up and round.*

JACKO: Would you like some snow?

JACK (*scandalized*): No!

JACKO: No?

PENELOPE: 'Snow'?

JACK: No!

JACKO: You'll have to wait till winter then. (*He is now swaggering.*)

    PENELOPE, *her splendid female confidence gone to the winds, backing before him. As he passes* JACK.

Music?

PENELOPE: Music?

JACK (*to* JACKO): Music yes.

    The bees roar. PENELOPE *looks up trips backwards – over the carcass perhaps – legs splayed. They freeze, the music cuts, she looking up at him, he down at her.* JACK *says softly to* JACKO, *with some reproach.*

Gently, darling, we've lots of time.

    PENELOPE, *furious, sits upright as* JACK *pulls* JACKO *gently away.*

PENELOPE: You *what*? (*Scrambling to her feet.*) Don't talk to *me* like that!

JACKO (*is sitting side by side with* JACK): Why not? That's how you talk to me.

    PENELOPE *is impressed and interested.* JACK *doesn't like this human rapport, gesturing that* PENELOPE *is to be dismissed, but* JACKO *and* PENELOPE *are absorbed in one another. She keeps a wary distance but doesn't move, speaks with a distinct note of self-exculpation.*

PENELOPE: You ask for it.

JACKO: No I don't.

PENELOPE: Well you seem to.

JACKO: Well I don't!

PENELOPE (*tries for a note of indifference*): . . . Coming back to the House?

JACKO (*luxuriant, leaning back on hands*): No.

PENELOPE: You're not going to stay here all week?

JACKO: Why not? The weather's good.

JACK (*aggrieved*): The weather's *mine*.

JACKO: Really?

PENELOPE (*alarmed by the double voice again, backing*): Jacko . . .?

JACKO (*turning to her*): You still here?

PENELOPE: What's happened to you, Jacko?

JACKO: I've been 'unbuttoned'——

JACK:——darling.

JACKO: Don't forget your dog.

> *This reminder completes her rout. She exits hastily, and as she goes they laugh as we have heard before:* HA HA HA HA HA HA HA. *As this choral barking collapses into individual mirth again, both are looking off after the retreating girl.* JACKO *still luxuriously sprawled,* JACK *crouched against him, face shining with spontaneous delight. For the moment they are simply friends.*

JACK: You *see*?

JACKO: Yes!

JACK: You frightened her!

JACKO (*modestly*): Oh not really.

JACK: You did. You're a *brute*! I thought you were gentle.

JACKO: I was.

JACK: Aye, and look where it got you!

JACKO: Aye. Thanks Jack.

JACK: *You* did it, Jacko.

JACKO: No Jack, credit where it's due.

JACK: Let's kill something else.

JACKO (*awkward*): . . . Kill what?

JACK: Well, anything, really. (*Looks back at his friend, anxiously and sad.*)

JACKO: Well . . . why?

JACK: I don't understand.

JACKO: What for?

JACK: I don't know what you mean!

JACKO: For what *reason*?

JACK: Oh stop it, please! . . . You don't want to.

JACKO: Well not for no reason.

JACK: You had me worried then.

> JACKO *looks at him warily. Reassuring.*

You're not a brute!

JACKO: You said I was.

JACK: I was *testing* you! A brute's no good to me – I need a human being.

JACKO: For what?

JACK: For King.

JACKO: And what's the King for?

JACK: To be gentle.

JACKO: I'm not gentle. Neither are you.

JACK (*coldly*): You've got it *half* right. I am. You're not.

> *As he says this a mass of white convolvulus and honeysuckle is lowered behind them. One of these* JACK *breaks off.*

(*Gravely*) I want you to smell this.

JACKO: Why?

JACK: Will you put your stubborn nose in it and try!

> JACKO *obeys.*

JACKO: It's ordinary woodbine.

JACK: There's no such thing.

> JACKO *returns his nose to the flower and at once the music starts, faintly, weird and seeking.* JACKO, *with an almost startled face is about to raise his nose from the flower, but eagerly.*

Go on!

> *The music finds whatever it was looking for. Coaxing.*

Now wander . . . Wander . . . (*Dryly.*) Travel a bit. 'Broaden' that 'mind' of yours . . .

> JACKO *is lost in the flower. Gently.*

I'm gentle, Jacko I did that. All this (*the Forest*), all freshness, lightness, brightness, mine. And Jacko, all true humbleness.

> JACKO *looks at him, he nods.*

Dogs – they snore by the fire and fart – that's humble. But their eyes shine, Jacko.

JACKO: Dogs——

JACK (*rising*):——fight. Yes, I know. Terribly considering their size; that terrible anxiety dogs fight with. But a dog with its teeth in another dog's throat is not so terrible, as a man in an office; and everyone knows this. And dogs are half-corrupted, dogs are tame – a lion now! What a machine! What a voice! Dignity! Mine too. Let's face it dear, you have lacked dignity . . . But with a box of matches any man can make a lion tremble. (*Sniggering.*) It's true – matches – dry sticks – fire, he slams his tail into its slot and soils himself! (*Snigger vanishes.*) And in that moment, with his effluence hot among his legs, he has more, oh much, a world more dignity, than the split, harsh thing, that lit the fire and doesn't know itself. All growth and strength. Oak beams hold up stone towers for generations! And who was ever hurt by the growing of an oak? (*But as he says this he spreads his hands as one who has nothing to hide, and they are crimson from his handling of the dog. He smiles foolishly and wipes them on his front, but there they leave stains which* JACKO's *eye still falls upon. Quickly pointing.*) Look! Look!

> *A bird's nest is lowered. He takes it. A bird whistles lyrically above them. They look up.*

She's not afraid. She knows me. Look.

JACKO (*smiling gravely*): . . . Thrush's eggs.

JACK: Yes. Look at them.

JACKO: Blue . . .

JACK: And fragile . . .

They are murmuring, heads together above the nest. He takes out delicately one of the eggs, the bird above whistles contentedly. Jacko, I did that.

JACKO (*indicating* JACK's *crimson palm*): And that. *Why?*

JACK: It was an accident.

JACKO: No.

JACK: To frighten Penelope!

JACKO: And if you're gentle, why frighten her?

Enter PENELOPE, *behind him.* JACK *seizes him so that he cannot turn and places a finger on his lips.*

PENELOPE (*gently*): Come back to the House, Jacko.

JACK (*gently*): No, darling.

PENELOPE: Please.

JACK: No, darling.

PENELOPE: All right . . .

Exit PENELOPE.

JACK: Did she ever speak to you like that before?

JACKO: Not since we were children.

JACK: Children! Oh you do catch on so quickly!

JACKO: Look I think I'll just go after her.

JACK: You'll lose her if you do! You're right. You didn't really frighten her. Oh no. You only borrowed . . . And if I—— (*Holding up his hands, palm towards* JACKO's *turned back he withdraws a step or two, delicately.*)

JACKO *shouts as one in peril.*

JACKO: Don't!

JACK: All right!

JACK *drops his hands.* JACKO *turns.*

JACKO: Good God, what did you do?

JACK: Good man I took back what you borrowed.

JACKO: What is it?

JACK: Me. And if you want her – do you want her?

JACKO: You know.

JACK: Well then you mustn't borrow it you must——

JACKO: Buy it.

JACK *cocks his head enquiringly.*

Buy. Pay for. Earn.

JACK (*aside*): Century by century they get steadily less intelligible. (*Back to* JACKO.) Do you want it?

JACKO: Don't deceive me Jack; there's something I must pay for it.

JACK: Nothing that I know of. (*This is evidently sincere.*)
     JACKO *thinks.*

JACKO: Something I must do for it?

JACK: Oh yes, you must do what you want.

JACKO: I daren't.
     JACKO *looks utterly sad.* JACK *smiles and pityingly pats him.*

JACK: Poor Jack, poor gentle Jack.

JACKO:—Jacko.

JACK:—Yes.

JACKO (*quietly, with a sigh*): Well . . . give me my glasses back. (*Holds out hand.*)

JACK: No! I've got a week. You're timid. Look, you won't take me on trust. You won't take you on trust. I'll tell you what you take on trust——

JACKO: What?

JACK: Other people. Right? Right. I'll make a bargain with you. Very handsome terms. Free of interest. Absolutely without obligation. Borrow for one week; and consult your other people. What d'you say?
     JACKO *is dubious.*

Terminable without notice!

JACKO: How?

JACK: Easy. Stay in the Forest, keep out of the House: as far as you're concerned you're me; as far as I'm concerned you're King. But! Leave the Forest, go into the House: as far as I'm concerned you've abdicated; as far as you're concerned I'm dead. But you undertake to ask the others if you should. The King has power to make fruit fall, insect song, other people happy, (*Much struck, righteous*)

that's what-d'you-call-it *Christian* that is! What d'you say?
The weather's warm, the ground's soft, Penelope will
bring you food.

JACKO *looks interested.*

She'll do whatever you want; of course she will; it's what
she wants; everyone doing what they want, it's the rule of
folly. (*Looks off again, cunningly dispassionate.*) And she's a
fine girl, we must have her.

JACKO: 'We'?

JACK (*testily*): You, you.

JACKO: You said 'we'.

JACK: Do you think I want her? Do you think there's anything of any sex, or shape, or size, that sweats in skin or
crawls in fur, on four legs or on two that I could any way
want for? And not have?

JACKO: You want me for something.

JACK (*goes to him, moved, takes his hands*): For your humanity.
Believe that, Jacko.

JACKO (*responding in kind*): I think I do, Jack.

JACK (*gravely*): You do.

JACKO: Yes.

   JACK *nods solemnly at* JACKO's *solemnity. He struggles.
No good. He is falling about the stage, helpless with wild mirth.
He flounders towards bewildered* JACKO, *claps him on the
shoulder. Gasps, by way of explanation.*

JACK: You're so *conceited*! (*He goes off into mirth again.*)

   Uncertainly JACKO *joins in.*

That's it Jacko laugh! 'And the world laughs with you'
doesn't it? Be me for a week you'll find you're generous.

   *He is insinuating him towards the exit as though all were
settled,* JACKO *smilingly resists; he desists and goes on smoothly.*
Be King, you'll find I'm cornucopia for *other* people too –
The Frenchman and his silly girl, the wretched married
couple——

JACKO: Dr Morgan?

JACK (*stopped*): What is that man?

JACKO: A mathematician.

JACK: Anathema——?

JACKO:—tician.

JACK: Oh yes. Like twice and a half and infinity. (*He is very still.*) He adds them up and tucks them in and pulls them out and arranges them. A mathematician, yes. I doubt there's much that we can do for Dr Morgan. (*Forced liveliness again.*) But all the others——!

JACKO: Miss Lazara?

JACK: Miss——?

JACKO: My boss.

JACK: Boss . . . (*Fatigued.*) Jacko, you're exhausting me.

JACKO: Why can't you be King yourself?

JACK: Thou fool . . . (*with ghastly bonhomie, hating him.*) Never mind, never mind you're cautious, that's only natural; and what could be more natural than to be – ha ha – natural? (*He is sweating with effort.*) I'm quite beside myself. (*He is standing side by side with* JACKO.) Really I am. Yes I know what you're – It's just that I'm – Well it's been such a long time – It's such a pleasure to meet anyone so . . . utterly . . . human! (*He falls silent.*)

> *They regard one another, separate again. A pause.*

So give me your hand. (*Holds out his own.*)

> JACKO *starts to hold out hand, hesitates.*

JACKO: Terminable?

JACK: Always terminable.

JACKO: Just by going into the House?

JACK: Just by doing that.

JACKO: Well on those terms . . .

JACK (*cheerfully and taking his hand*): What have you got to lose?

JACKO (*as soon as they clasp hands, richly emboldened*): Nothing!

> *And in the same instant the insects suddenly hum to signalize the bargain.* JACK *releases him and fusses with his garlands,*

JACKO *impatient to be gone, like a horse and its owner before the race.*

JACK: I'll see you on the Seventh Day.

JACKO: You're not coming?

JACK: No, you take it with you. And if at the end of the week you want it——

JACKO: Yes——?

JACK: Well then you've got it haven't you?

JACKO: So I have.

JACK: One small thing – don't muck about with the weather.

JACKO: Why not?

JACK: Don't know.

JACKO: What if it rains?

JACK: It won't. Be gentle, Jack.

JACKO: I've got it.

JACK: Not *too* gentle.

JACKO: I've *got* it. (*And he brushes away* JACK's *hand.*)

JACK (*laughing at his impatience*): Off you go then! Lovely lad!

Exit JACKO. JACK's *smile fades. Suddenly emits an involuntary exclamation like one who gets the aftertaste of foul food.*

JACK: Yau-augh! (*Absently he picks up the bird's nest.*) The conceit . . . (*Looks out over audience. Wonderingly.*) By everything that's liquid – the constructed, rigid, storeyed, climbing, cloud-compelling, star-obscuring, scaffolded conceit! Of the species. (*Looks at the bird's nest.*) So it is though . . . it's got to be a human.

Going, not savagely but with perfect carelessness he tosses the nest from him and the bird's distraught shrieking clatters from above as he exits. The stage darkens to night and moonlight; then the light comes up again for day, but another piece of foliage has flown away, the House is a little more revealed and enter VIOLET, MORGAN, CHAMPION, CHAUFFEUR. MORGAN *with handbag and gloves.*

VIOLET: An additional day and night I've wasted here at your

request already. When he does turn up you may tell him
that he is dismissed.

MORGAN: Twenty-four hours; wasted; one after the other

VIOLET: Not twenty-four, seventy-two. Twenty-four of
mine, twenty-four of Mr Champion's, twenty-four of his
not his, mine! His are bought and paid for.

MORGAN: Hours are not commodities. You are affronted
that it's all.

VIOLET: He made a bargain. He undertook to be where he
was wanted and to do what he was told. He accepted
payment for it! Confound it, may I not defend myself? Mr
Champion!

CHAMPION: The principle is unassailable; but I share Dr
Morgan's concern for young Cadence.

VIOLET: Concern? Why yes, he's concerned!

MORGAN: The boy has been tipped into some kind of crisis

VIOLET: The young man has stolen a holiday. Morgan he's
rattled you.

MORGAN: He's rattled us both; you're being mean-minded

VIOLET: I can't employ him; it's a bargain which he's
broken.

MORGAN: Is that an unforgivable sin?

VIOLET: Not a sin of any sort, a fact. Forgiveness doesn't
mend it.

MORGAN: I anticipate you'll take a more generous view in
the event.

VIOLET: Then you anticipate a revolution, in my nature.

Exit VIOLET, CHAMPION, CHAUFFEUR. *Another piece of
foliage flies, further revealing House and also* GASTON *and*
CYNTHIA. *Their attitude to* MORGAN *is amused.* MORGAN
calls; softly.

MORGAN: Jacko!

CYNTHIA: Hubert says his sister says that Mr Cadence spoke
to her.

MORGAN (*sees them, unruffled by their attitude*): When?

GASTON: Last night.

CYNTHIA: His second night out.

GASTON: She told him he should stay out.

MORGAN: At night. With – that girl?

CYNTHIA: Marigold. Yes. Marigold's impressed.

MORGAN (*leaving them*): He asks advice of a village whore. Me he avoids.

CYNTHIA: Are you looking for him, Dr Morgan?

MORGAN: I think he'd better be found.

> *Exit* MORGAN. *As he goes* GASTON *and* CYNTHIA *laugh as we have heard before,* 'Ha Ha Ha Ha Ha Ha Ha' *but tinklingly and comfortable.* JACKO *enters behind them.*

JACKO: That's a sound I like to hear.

GASTON (*startled*): Jacko!

> JACKO *looks at* CYNTHIA.

JACKO: You look very nice.

> *He performs the statutory road-house mimicry of desire, a dog-like growling and pawing of the ground with one foot.*

G–rrrr–rr!

GASTON (*amused surprise*): Jacko!

JACKO: Jack.

GASTON: But of course! You are King of the Woods! You benefit I think.

JACKO: That's what Marigold said.

GASTON: Oh yes. We heard that you met Marigold . . . Formidable!

JACKO (*bending towards him from the waist, and by way of a delicate compliment to* GASTON's *nationality*): Le mot juste. Ha!

> CYNTHIA *has been watching him with increasing interest, and now, protestingly:*

CYNTHIA: Isn't she awfully dirty?

JACKO (*off hand*): Dirty? Yes, she's dirty. (*To* GASTON *behind his hand.*) But what hams!

GASTON: Jacko – do I understand that you and Marigold . . . ?

JACKO: No. (*Assertive.*) I pinched her bottom!

GASTON: Bravo!

JACKO: But no . . . No . . . No . . . Not with Marigold. Cynthia's right. She's dirty.

CYNTHIA: Penelope is looking for you.

JACKO (*quickly*): She is?

GASTON: *She* thinks you benefit too!

JACKO: She does?

GASTON: Oh yes!

JACKO: Then that's all right. (*Briskly, as one who turns to the business of the day.*) Now how about you——?

GASTON:——Mm?

JACKO:——Have you got her into bed yet?

He jerks his head familiarly towards CYNTHIA *who can hear all this.* GASTON *stares and then, displeased on her behalf, his smile quite gone:*

GASTON: . . . Now one moment my friend——

JACKO:——Ah, you haven't. Cynthia, a word in your ear.

He steps away from him, beckoning CYNTHIA *to accompany him. She is acquiescent, but——*

GASTON: Monsieur!

He steps between them, now smiling very artificially, and all the more formidable for his tone of mild explication.

You are taking a very high hand.

JACKO: It becomes me to. Cynthia——

He deftly negotiates GASTON *who, exasperated, grips him by the arm and still more mildly but now quite definitely threatening.*

GASTON: Understand me. You extend your little joke a little far.

Very slowly, JACKO *turns a face of lamb-like mildness upon* GASTON. *The bees murmur sweetly, though unheard.* GASTON *loosens his grip and backs away, and backs away again bewildered and unnerved by whatever he has glimpsed in* JACKO. *Sharply, warningly:*

Cynthia! Cynthia - come away!

CYNTHIA: Why?

GASTON: Cynthia!

But JACKO *turns the same face slowly towards her and her reaction is an intimate smile.*

CYNTHIA: You *have – changed*, Jacko.

The bees stop.

JACKO: Yes I have. You haven't. Now why?

CYNTHIA (*smiling*): I'm frightened.

JACKO (*smiling*): But that's the main attraction.

CYNTHIA (*smiling*): Yes.

JACKO: One moment.

He goes to GASTON, *turning him about.*

I sense no insurmountable reluctance? You're dilatory Monsieur; this weather isn't going to last for ever.

GASTON (*hesitates, then shrugs, grumpily*): It is something the old Lazara has said.

JACKO: Miss *Lazara?*

GASTON: The young girl consults the old woman. This is usual. And usually, fruitful; but this time no. Why I do not know; because she will not tell me what Miss Lazara has said!

JACKO: Come.

He draws GASTON *back towards* CYNTHIA *she is looking vulnerable as they advance.*

What did Miss Lazara say?

CYNTHIA: She said it was a bargain——

JACKO:—Bargain!

CYNTHIA:—bargain I could only make the once and I should get the best terms possible!

GASTON: Best terms! In terms of what?

CYNTHIA: Pleasure!

GASTON (*enchanted*): We-e-e-ell . . .! A wise old woman. She is absolutely right.

But JACKO *has withdrawn.*

JACKO: I used to work for her . . . Wise? Yes, it cannot have escaped your notice Cynthia that this 'bargain' is a bargain which Miss Lazara has so far been unable to negotiate, for herself. Wisdom prevents; I recommend folly. Wisdom is knowledge and knowledge is power and Miss Lazara's powerful. But power is possession and having and being are separate modes; knowing and doing are separate modes. So Cynthia, will you have your life or live it? Will you *do* what you want or will you, like Miss Lazara, be self-possessed?

He has moved back to CYNTHIA, *standing between her and* GASTON.

GASTON: Bravo!

CYNTHIA (*to* JACKO): Don't tell me *he's* not self-possessed.

JACKO (*to* CYNTHIA): Gaston is a special case. Across the Channel they have the knack of knowing what they want. And he wants you. We on the other hand know *or* want. Do you want him?

There is intimacy and trust between them, they are speaking quietly. She peeps round him at GASTON, *looks back at him. Seriously:*

CYNTHIA: I don't know.

JACKO: Excellent. Come along then. (*He takes her gently by the wrist and leads her to the bench or rostrum, which he mounts, collecting* GASTON *on the way.*) I will now pronounce you man and woman. Gaston Pascal Descartes Dupont, do you want this woman?

GASTON: I do!

JACKO: Cynthia Elizabeth, Elizabeth Dalrymple, do you – What's the matter dear?

She has pulled herself free of his grip, he immediately loosing it.

CYNTHIA: Does he love me?

JACKO: Oh, Cynthia, don't burden your *heart* with it . . . the weather's warm, the ground is soft; all the other animals are happy.

He holds out his hand, but she hesitates; he takes back his own hand; a swift consideration, then:

Monsieur, might I suggest——? (*Turning him about.*) Back to back.

    CYNTHIA *acquiesces.*

(*discreetly*) The presence of the other person is often an embarrassment.

GASTON: Jacko! Where did you learn all this?

    JACKO *hesitates and then, to* CYNTHIA, *softly:*

JACKO: He's missed the whole point, hasn't he?

CYNTHIA (*now looking at him quite adoringly*): I don't know what you're talking about.

JACKO: A very good sign. I'm saying, Cynthia, that since you began to count your days you haven't been a child. I'm right about that am I? The clock has started?

CYNTHIA: Yes.

JACKO: Tick tock. If you count them you must live them. Life won't live them for you any more. Tick tock in any case. *Do*, darling, or you're playing leapfrog with a skeleton. Not now, too late; back over back; out of youth, through middle-age, to ugliness; and one day – plop – too late; the girl's gone; the skeleton stands upright, and the earth starts sliding.

GASTON: Horrible!

CYNTHIA: Horrible ...

    JACKO *stoops to* CYNTHIA's *upturned face.*

GASTON: Cynthia.

CYNTHIA: Jacko.

JACKO: Gaston.

CYNTHIA (*obediently*): Gaston.

JACKO: Commence Monsieur.

GASTON: If I am self-possessed my Cynthia, release me.

JACKO: Very good.

GASTON: Please!

JACKO: Sorry.

    He is carefully steering CYNTHIA's *hand towards* GASTON's, *which is groping for it; when they meet they link galvanically.*

CYNTHIA: Yes!

GASTON: The weather's warm——

CYNTHIA: The ground's soft——

GASTON: Let's be happy.

CYNTHIA: Yes . . . *Will* it make me happy?

GASTON: Yes.

CYNTHIA: Then why'm I frightened?

GASTON: Are you frightened?

CYNTHIA: Yes.

GASTON: I will be gentle.

JACKO: Not *too* gentle!

GASTON: Jacko! Thank you! But enough!

> *Gathers* CYNTHIA *and makes swiftly off Upstage.*

JACKO: Well – there's gratitude!

> *Clicks fingers; a lemon falls Frontstage which he catches.*

JACKO: Hey!

> *Holds out the lemon between finger and thumb towards* CYNTHIA. *She comes for it.*

For half-time.

CYNTHIA: Thank you Jacko.

> *Takes the lemon, which, however, he does not relinquish.*

JACKO: How'm I doing?

CYNTHIA: Fine . . . just fine.

JACKO: You don't think I should come inside then?

CYNTHIA: Oh no . . . !

> GASTON *now comes forward; with controlled impatience:*

GASTON: By no means. You enjoy yourself. It was high time. Congratulations. (*Disengaging their mutual grasp upon the lemon.*) Thank you. (*Takes* CYNTHIA *off again.*) Gratitude! Felicitations! But enough!

> *Exit* GASTON *and* CYNTHIA.

JACKO: Ha!

> *He makes a triumphant flourish and the* MUSIC *starts and the light change* DAY – NIGHT – DAY *begins. He struts happily Frontstage, admires himself.*

Who would have thought that the young man had so much blood in him? I have been waiting for myself. I have been twenty-seven years in prison. And I step out, undiminished, and with not a mark on me! . . . I must contain, some marvellous preservative. (*Walks, is arrested by a terrible thought.*) I might have lived for seventy years, and died entire . . . it's very shocking.

The lighting change complete, enter BRACKETS, *hand in hand.*

BRACKET: Have you sent it?

She pulls a crumpled letter, stamped and addressed, from the pocket of her skirt.

MRS BRACKET: Needs a new envelope.

BRACKET (*friendly*): Don't stick your stomach out, Joy.

MRS BRACKET: Sorry. (*Looks down; evidently makes a fruitless effort for:*) Won't go in.

BRACKET (*self-reprobatory*): Sorry.

MRS BRACKET: No, it's unsightly. Sorry.

BRACKET: Sorry.

JACKO: I'll help them.

They see him and at once go into their boisterous social routine.

BRACKET: Hello! Mr Cadence!

MRS BRACKET: Jacko! *Hello* there!

JACKO *crosses, his expression serious and sympathetic.*

JACKO: No, no, no. There's no necessity.

He clasps his hands behind his back.

Now what's holding up this divorce?

An astounded silence.

BRACKET: Who says we want a divorce?

JACKO (*he looks only at the woman, and that intimately*): Don't you?

MRS BRACKET: We don't seem to.

JACKO: You derive what you want from what you do? That's topsy-turvy.

BRACKET (*truculently*): Is it?

MRS BRACKET: Yes.

JACKO *nods approvingly.* BRACKET *is bewildered and uneasy at their rapport.*

BRACKET: Well I say: Twenty years of doing something is a better guide to what you want than what you say you want!

JACKO: Who said that, Miss Lazara?

BRACKET: Yes.

JACKO: She would. She lives on other people's regularity. So far as we can think of her as living, poor, deprived lady.

MRS BRACKET: Jacko!

JACKO *takes the letter from her. With a gasp of indignation* BRACKET *snatches for it but his wife arrests his hand.* JACKO *holds the letter at a distance from his face.*

JACKO: I haven't got my spectacles ... Mmmm ... Even here you see, you practically invite the man to talk you out of it.

BRACKET: Now just one minute——

He snatches the letter from JACKO's *grasp with such impetuosity that* MRS BRACKET *is thrown off balance. It is genuine violence but* JACKO *faces him with total calm. There is a momentary tableau. In the silence:*

JACKO: Did Miss Lazara have anything to say about twenty years of doing nothing? Because that's the problem isn't it ...

BRACKET *releases his tense posture and looks away.* JACKO *gives a philosophic sigh.*

That's the problem ... (*and abruptly brisk, inspiriting and sensible, he leads the linked pair Upstage saying*) Let's see if we can't find out a little more about this.

He has brought them to the place where he conducted the nuptials of GASTON *and* CYNTHIA, *and as though this were some consulting room.*

Sit down.

She sits and being linked, he must, perforce.

Now – without too much thought – what's the difficulty?

BRACKET: The difficulty is we're married!

JACKO: Well done, I don't think this is going to take us long. In 1943 you made a contract, verbal but witnessed and legally binding——

BRACKET (*contemptuous*): That's not the point.

JACKO: I don't mean it's a matter for the police.

BRACKET: It's not the point at all.

MRS BRACKET: We were married in church.

JACKO: Do you believe in God?

MRS BRACKET } (*together*): No.
BRACKET }

JACKO: Then that's not the point.

MRS BRACKET: We promised to love one another . . .

JACKO: You promised more than you could answer for.

BRACKET (*thumping the floor*): We meant it!

MRS BRACKET: My parents were there. My sister came from Canada. We had 'Jesu Joy of Man's Desiring'.

JACKO:——But! You promised to desire each other. Till death did you part. Death's not done that. You're still joined. Do you still desire each other?

The BRACKETS *slightly turn their lowered heads and look at one another from the corners of their eyes. They let go one another's hands. He wipes his on his seat, she on her handkerchief.* JACKO *seizes this opportunity by taking* BRACKET'*s wrist and drawing him aside but he resists.*

BRACKET: You can't just walk away from someone, Jacko.

JACKO: Why?

BRACKET: We've been married twenty years.

JACKO: So?

BRACKET: Oh don't be daft . . . all that time, she's cooked my food; she's made my bed; she's washed my clothes; she's – dressed my gammy leg! She's – wiped my razor! She's talked to me. I'm obligated.

JACKO: Obligated.

BRACKET: Yes. She's been a good wife!

JACKO: Wait.

> *Crosses to* MRS BRACKET.

Joy——

MRS BRACKET: He's considerate; he's reliable; he's generous – he's given me my keep for twenty years and hasn't even noticed he was doing it; he's been patient; he's been pleasant; he's even been amusing; and he's never been unfaithful.

JACKO (*quietly*): Don't you wish he had?

MRS BRACKET: You're young Jacko.

JACKO: You're not old.

MRS BRACKET: Leave me alone! He's been a good husband.

JACKO: And you're obligated.

MRS BRACKET: Yes!

> JACKO *backs from them Upstage, smiling benevolently.*

JACKO: I have good news for you Brackets——

> *They stare lumpishly——*

Have an apple! Have a pear!

> *Clicks two thumbs and fingers; two fruits fall.*

BRACKET: Where did those come from?

JACKO: The Hesperides! Brackets! *Desire* each other? (*Generously.*) You don't even like each other!

> *But the* BRACKETS *expostulate; they threaten to come together.* JACKO *gets between them and, the* MUSIC *diminishing, patrols from one to the other with his hands behind his back, something like a barrister:*

Joy – Stirling, eat your pear – Joy, is it not a fact that Stirling's teeth – click?

MRS BRACKET: He can't help that!

JACKO: He's helpless in the matter.

MRS BRACKET: Yes!

JACKO: And does that make his clicking less abrasive to your nerves? Or more?

> *She stares at him; he nods and turns away.*

Stirling, does not Joy, not from motives of economy but of set intent, keep fragments of cheese, half tomatoes and single slices of cold pork in separate, transparent polythene bags, each superfluously labelled?

BRACKET: . . . Well, yes, she does.

JACKO: And how does this affect you?

BRACKET *will not answer but suddenly rubs his face with nervous violence.*

Quite so. Joy – do you or do you not borrow from the library and affect to read books beyond your intellectual station——?

She darkly bites her apple.

And is her conversation not in consequence at once humiliating and inadequate?

BRACKET: Now that's true . . . (*and slowly bites his apple*).

JACKO: Stirling. When Joy is provocatively rude to you——

BRACKET: Yes?

JACKO: Do not you most viciously forgive her, sometimes before guests?

MRS BRACKET: He does! He does!

BRACKET (*grinning sheepishly*): I know what you mean.

JACKO: None of that! You mind your own business . . . Joy, what is Stirling's attitude to strangers?

MRS BRACKET:—?

JACKO: Strangers in large cars.

MRS BRACKET: Smarmy.

JACKO: And how is this expressed?

MRS BRACKET: He wags his tail!

BRACKET: I *what*?

JACKO: A sort of undulation of the rear parts, Stirling, I've noticed it myself.

BRACKET: Oh well, if we're going to be personal——

JACKO: Oh no, it's not a physical infirmity. (*To her.*) It is a—? (*Breaking off like an oral examiner.*)

MRS BRACKET: Spiritual give-away!

BRACKET: Oh here we go – the Life of the Mind!

MRS BRACKET: My word he's coarse!

BRACKET: My word she's pretentious!

MRS BRACKET: Oh Honest John! He smiles in the mirror!

BRACKET: She talks to herself!

MRS BRACKET (*shocked*): I don't——

> *As soon as the thing is well under way,* JACKO *takes the letter and a pen from* BRACKET'*s pocket and using* BRACKET'*s back as a lectern makes brisk alterations to the letter, applying himself thoughtfully, while:*

BRACKET: You do. You're unhappy!

MRS BRACKET: You don't wash your hands! You eat like a dog! You've got varicose veins!

BRACKET: You talk to yourself.

MRS BRACKET: You're *dull*!

BRACKET: You're unhappy.

MRS BRACKET: You're lazy in bed!

BRACKET: I'm bored in bed!

MRS BRACKET: It's all that hot milk!

BRACKET: It's those interlock nighties!

MRS BRACKET: You're one of the boys! You miss your mother! You only know two jokes, and they're both about the R.A.F.!

BRACKET: Joy, Joy——

MRS BRACKET: Yes?

BRACKET: I've read your diary!

MRS BRACKET: Stirling!

BRACKET: Joy!

> *They run together joining hands.*

You don't like me!

MRS BRACKET (*radiant*): I hate you!

BRACKET (*radiant*): I hate you too!

MRS BRACKET: No harm done then!

BRACKET: None at all!

> JACKO *approaches, conning his letter.*

JACKO: There we are, a little grubby, but the intention's plain. Ah – ah! Don't lean on it. (*Unlinks their hands.*)

All laugh.

Who'll have it?

MRS BRACKET: } I will.
BRACKET: }

JACKO: You. (*Gives the letter to her.*) You're happy then?

MRS BRACKET: I've lost ten years! Fifteen!

JACKO: Then go your ways!

They go, Left and Right.

Dear separated Brackets, your lovely, separate ways. And flowers spring in your paths!

At exits they pause.

BRACKET: Aren't you coming in?

JACKO: You think I should?

MRS BRACKET: Penelope's looking for you.

JACKO: She'll find me then.

BRACKET: Dr Morgan's having kittens.

JACKO: Indeed? Who's the lucky Tom?

BRACKET: Jacko, what's got into you?

JACKO: You wouldn't believe me if I told you.

MRS BRACKET: Well I say he should stick it out!

BRACKET: Aye do! It's only three more days!

JACKO: I will then. Jolly good luck to you Brackets!

BRACKET: Jolly good luck to *you*!

JACKO (*harsh jocosity*): Jolly good luck to us all!

The stage is plunged from day to night.

Exit BRACKET. MRS BRACKET *speaks from the shadows.*

MRS BRACKET: Why Mr Cadence . . .

JACKO: What?

MRS BRACKET: You sounded like your father . . .

MRS TREADGOLD (*off, sharp, alarmed*): Mr Cadence!

Exit MRS BRACKET. *Enter* MRS TREADGOLD. *She moves timidly into the area of light, looks up at vine-leaved* JACKO *and asks:*

G

Have you gone mad?

JACKO: Is that what they say?

MRS TREADGOLD: They say you've improved out of all recognition.

TREADGOLD (*off*): My dear?

MRS TREADGOLD: I've found him!

Enter TREADGOLD. *He and his wife stand together humbly.*

MRS TREADGOLD: He isn't mad. Dear Mr Cadence come back to the House. Let me tell Penelope to go back home. And you will call on her tomorrow. Properly. I disapprove of matchmaking but, I think Penelope will take you.

They smile at one another.

JACKO: Then I think I'll take Penelope. Why not? After all, I must be the only able-bodied man in Monmouthshire who hasn't!

MRS TREADGOLD: Oh Mr Cadence that's not what I meant! You know it's not! What's happened to you, Jacko?

JACKO: I met Jack.

Silence.

MRS TREADGOLD *backs towards her husband.*

MRS TREADGOLD: That's what Cedric said.

JACKO: Did you, Cedric?

TREADGOLD: Speaking metaphorically.

JACKO: Speaking what?

JACKO *jumps down.* MRS TREADGOLD *starts backwards, falls with a cry.* JACKO, *concerned, steps towards her, but with a gasp of fear she throws up an arm to ward him off. Shocked he stops.*

JACKO: Oh Mrs Treadgold . . . Metaphorically . . . Metaphorically.

The foliage shivers; the bees moan.

JACKO *sits on the bench, head sunk, troubled, while* TREADGOLD *assists his wife to her feet. A silence.*

MRS TREADGOLD: Mr Cadence?

JACKO: I'm tired.

MRS TREADGOLD: You've been out here five days Mr
  Cadence. It's too much of a strain.

JACKO: I didn't ask to be elected.

MRS TREADGOLD: We did wrong.

JACKO: Did you? She never looked for me before.

MRS TREADGOLD: You were inept with her. I say it with
  shame: sometimes you made me angry, you were so inept.
  But Mr Cadence you were always *kind*. Now, there's
  something *cruel* in you which I never saw before! And the
  week's been so strange! The weather's so hot! And the
  Brackets have parted! (*Braces herself.*) In the House, you
  could, canoodle.

JACKO (*is amused and touched. Hesitating*): Is she in the House
  now?

MRS TREADGOLD: She is looking through the Forest for
  you like an animal.

TREADGOLD: Let her find you.

MRS TREADGOLD: Cedric . . .?

TREADGOLD: And don't listen to my wife.

MRS TREADGOLD (*quickly*): I'll go now.

  And quickly she exits. TREADGOLD *speaks.*

TREADGOLD: Take her while you want her. While your
  need lasts she'll need you. Mr Cadence, like that life's all
  brilliance and freedom. And it's the brief way to her; that
  short connection is the only one. Kindness . . . lights little
  lonely fires, that twinkle across miles of black indifference
  . . . I know . . .

  After a moment he exits, still not looking at JACKO *who
  stares after him, begins to smile, to laugh as we have heard before:*
  Ha Ha Ha Ha Ha Ha Ha! *As his laughter dies away he is
  sprawled luxuriously on the bench, and* GRIEVES, *entering with
  another.*

GRIEVES: Having a little holiday are you sir?

JACKO: I'm not working.

GRIEVES: That's right sir.

JACKO: It's not the same thing Grieves.

GRIEVES: It is sir, when you've got a job to go back to sir.

JACKO: At eighty quid a week eh?

GRIEVES: That's right sir.

JACKO: Why do you lather me with 'sirs'?

GRIEVES: I'm paid to.

JACKO: *Eight* a week.

GRIEVES: That's right sir.

JACKO: 'T isn't *my* fault.

GRIEVES: Yes sir, it is.

JACKO: No, it's not!

GRIEVES: Yes sir it is. Let's say you're worth more than me sir; are you worth ten times as much?

JACKO: No of course not.

GRIEVES: I wouldn't say so either sir. So why does a careful lady like Miss Lazara pay it? Because you're standing on my neck! . . . That's what you're paid for. Beg pardon sir, could we have that bench?

  JACKO rises, *somewhat shaken, the* SECOND SERVANT *at a nod from* GRIEVES *approaches and prepares to lift the other end of the bench.*

JACKO: I haven't got a job – I've got the sack.

GRIEVES: The sack sir? Whatever's that?

JACKO: Don't you know?

GRIEVES: What it is sir? No. I know what it feels like.

SECOND SERVANT: Like losing an arm Mr Cadence——!

GRIEVES: Shurrup! (*He nods curtly; they carry off bench, he saying*) That how it feels to you sir?

JACKO (*calling*): No. Like losing a rupture!

GRIEVES (*returning*): That's not the sack sir. That's a holiday.

JACKO: You make me sick.

GRIEVES: Yes sir.

JACKO: Oh Grieves – on a night like this – can't you feel how . . . inadequate, all this is?

GRIEVES: I feel that all the time sir. (*At exit, pauses.*) Might

I ask you not to tell Miss Lazara that I make you sick sir? She'd give me the sack.

JACKO: You're a great little hater, aren't you?

GRIEVES: Yes sir, I am. (*Going.*)

JACKO: Grieves.

GRIEVES: Sir?

JACKO: Have an apple.

He clicks his fingers. Nothing happens. He looks up, does it again and again nothing happens. GRIEVES *watches poker-faced, then:*

GRIEVES: You want to be careful, sir.

Exit GRIEVES. JACKO, *worried, clicks again. Again nothing happens; the power has left him. He calls:*

JACKO: Jack? . . . Jack? . . . Jack?

A voice calls, off:

VOICE (*off*): Jacko!

JACKO: Penelope?

Enter MORGAN.

MORGAN: No, not Penelope. (*Moves into the light.*) It is now time to break this gesture off.

JACKO: Why?

MORGAN: It lacks all measure! One day, two days, very well you administer a little fright and no doubt they're the better for it——

JACKO:——I'm the better for it.

MORGAN: No. You are not.

JACKO: I am and you don't like it.

MORGAN (*after a pause*): I have nothing to do with it. (*He walks determinedly to Exit but stops.*) You were calling. For whom were you calling?

JACKO: Jack.

MORGAN: Unless one's only partly in possession of one's wit one does not call, materially, physically *call* for a metaphor!

JACKO: No.

MORGAN: Jacko do you think me sane?

JACKO: Yes.

MORGAN: Then there is such a thing as sanity.

JACKO: Yes.

MORGAN: The concept sanity implies the possibility of madness! For God's sake boy come back to the House – I don't know who or what you fancy you are in communion with – but——

JACKO: Who.

MORGAN peers at him clinically.

It's a who.

MORGAN: *What's* a who? Jacko, what is? What?

JACKO: Oh Morgan . . . the metaphor.

Again the foliage shivers; the bees moan.

JACKO sits, dispiritedly: MORGAN *walks about aimlessly before fetching up to say:*

MORGAN: She'll find you in the House as easily as here.

JACKO's gaze wanders:

(*impatiently barks*): Come into the House!

JACKO looks at him. A pause.

JACKO: That sounds like an order.

MORGAN: It is!

Another pause.

JACKO: Then go to Hell.

MORGAN exits.

Thoughtfully JACKO *clicks his fingers. But he does not look up. He calls. But is experimental.*

Jack? (*He rises. He calls now urgently. He clicks and clicks again, looking up.*) Jack. If you will just—Jack? Jack! Please.

JACK enters unseen behind him, stands looking at him coldly as JACKO *releases a whole fusillade of clickings.* JACKO *senses him, turns, starts a little at the basilisk quality of* JACK's *glare, the unwonted dignity of his stance.* JACK *slowly raises his hand, clicks his fingers once. A fusillade of apples descends upon* JACKO's *head.*

JACK: There is no need for you to speak of me. But if you do, don't deny me. (*Advancing, indignant.*) That filthy creature that thinks I'm a metaphor – the mathematician?

JACKO: Yes?

JACK: Your friend?

JACKO: Yes?

JACK: The one you wanted me to help?

JACKO: Yes!

JACK: You dirty little object.

JACKO: He's a very nice man!

JACK: I'm sorry to have to tell you this, Jacko: That man's a monster. Keep away from him. There now, I've warned you, haven't I? . . . (*Brisk.*) Well now, that leaves, Miss Lazara – Ah, here she comes.

JACKO: Miss Lazara?

PENELOPE (*off*): Jacko!

JACK: Penelope. (*Invites* JACKO *with a gesture to join her.*) I'll see you tomorrow. The Seventh Day.

PENELOPE (*off*): Jacko!

JACK: Make use of me.

PENELOPE (*off*): Jacko!

> JACKO *backs warily from* JACK, *suddenly turns and Exits, crying on a note of relief.*

JACKO: Penelope!

JACK: And I'll attend, to the Boss.

> *Saying which he patrols the perimeter of the Stage, holding up one hand, causing the Forest to fly away and the Office window to replace the House, while Clerks enter with Office furniture, and Exit,* SECRETARY *remaining.* JACK *undoes button of* SECRETARY'*s jacket.* SECRETARY *does it up again and places cards on table ready for business ritual.* JACK *undoes the button again and moves the cards from left to right. Takes a leaf from his tunic and places it on table, Exits as* VIOLET *enters opposite with* CHAMPION, *he saying:*

CHAMPION: This extraordinary weather has pursued us to the City.

SECRETARY: Good morning.

VIOLET: Perhaps you would prefer to take your jacket *off*, Mr Kent?

    SECRETARY, *startled, fastens button.*

Good morning. These (*the cards*) should not be here, they should be here! (*To* CHAMPION.) What?

CHAMPION: The weather.

VIOLET: I hadn't noticed. However, this morning the lift attendants were not attending to their lifts, I find my records strewn about my desk like so much orange peel and Mr Kent attired for the sea-side! No doubt the weather is to blame. There is nothing from Mexico?

CHAMPION: Nothing. (*Begins ritual.*) Starfire.

VIOLET: Nothing.

CHAMPION: Fairterm.

VIOLET: Nothing.

CHAMPION: King and Consort.

VIOLET: Nothing.

CHAMPION: Starfire Second Chance.

VIOLET: Nothing.

CHAMPION: Bullion.

    Enter JACK *magically 'drawing'* BILBO *after him.*

VIOLET: Godammit you've done it again!

BILBO (*harshly*): Yes.

    At his tone, SECRETARY *and* CHAMPION *exit,* CHAMPION *looking back at* BILBO, JACK *exits opposite.*

VIOLET: You have bought back my hotels?

BILBO: Those were my 'orders'.

VIOLET: Show me.

    He scribbles a figure. She looks.

No.

BILBO: He wouldn't sell for less. Why should he?

VIOLET: Oh no. Oh no no. No Bilbo, this time – you're sacked!

BILBO: Not now, too late, I've resigned.

VIOLET: Plyah!

BILBO: Oh yes. I left my letter in the outer office.

She sees that this is true. Moreover his manner is increasingly easy.

VIOLET: You're going to work for someone else.

BILBO: Yes. Myself.

VIOLET: Hah! You're going to be a broker!

BILBO: No. I'll work in my own property.

VIOLET: You have no property.

BILBO: Not much. A block of Quantox Preferential.

VIOLET: How much?

BILBO: A hundred thousand.

VIOLET: Where is it?

BILBO: Mexico.

VIOLET: A 'gift'.

BILBO: Yes.

VIOLET: You gave to Signor Santa Cruz for those precarious hotels, seven millions sterling of my money and he gave you a hundred thousand Quantox.

BILBO: Yes.

VIOLET: Conspiracy to fraud.

BILBO: Not quite.

VIOLET: I'll show it so in court.

BILBO: No. Not against him in a Mexican court.

VIOLET: Blackguard.

BILBO: Oh, Violet . . .!

VIOLET: A block of Quantox; you're right; it isn't much.

BILBO: It's enough. In ten years' time I'll buy you out.

VIOLET: Blackguard! You must have 'made yourself agreeable' to Signor Santa Cruz.

BILBO: I did——

VIOLET:——I can imagine——

BILBO:——Can you——?

VIOLET:——At the bull-fight——

BILBO: And other places.

VIOLET: Blackguard! Yo-o-o-ou . . . urchin! (*Calls.*)

Champion! Ten years' time? I hope I'm dead in ten years' time. Champion!

Enter CHAMPION.

VIOLET: Ascertain if Mr Cubit's deal with Santa Cruz is actual.

BILBO: The money's in his bank.

VIOLET: I gave you too much power.

BILBO: You never gave me any!

VIOLET: Get out!

BILBO: I'm going!

VIOLET: Go then!

BILBO: Yes!

But neither moves.

VIOLET: Greedy, greedy, guttersnipe!

BILBO: From you! 'Greedy'! When did you part with anything?

VIOLET: I give away more money than you know how to want.

BILBO: No, anything . . . Anything, Violet.

VIOLET:—Get out——!

BILBO:—Money's nothing.

VIOLET: From you!

BILBO: Stupid woman.

VIOLET: Now I'll strike you. I'll strike you!

But he flinches not at all and smiles at her.

You could have had it all! Get out! What did you want? You could have had it all.

BILBO: I wanted——

VIOLET: Get out!

He is going.

Help me.

He stops.

Quickly.

He approaches, she turns away in fear, knocks the cards on the floor. He kneels and gathers them.

Oh leave them, leave them! Bilbo please!

   Unmoved he continues.

My old ideas are collecting . . . Bilbo quickly tell me something new.

BILBO (*rising sternly*): Me? Maybe some old, old man somewhere could tell you something you don't know. Not me.

VIOLET (*smiling*): I love . . . your cruelty.

BILBO: I wanted, Independence, Power, You.

VIOLET: In that order?

BILBO: They wouldn't come in any other order. So I took, the first.

VIOLET: You mean, that you will take, the other two?

BILBO: If I'm lucky.

VIOLET: You are lucky, Bilbo. But it cannot be so. (*Sits.*) Look at my hand!

BILBO: It's a good hand.

VIOLET: It has a good shape, but that's with handling money. The skin is good but that's cosmetics. It shakes! The sinews stare! The veins are glassy, and that's my age! It cannot be that you want that.

BILBO: I've taken what I wanted.

VIOLET: You took a miserable clutch of shabby shares!

BILBO (*patiently*): Which have made me, Independent.

VIOLET: . . . Oh . . . I see . . . (*A tentative smile of dawning hope.*)

BILBO: Well then remember it. For both our sakes.

VIOLET: And what will you do? Now?

BILBO: You must wait on the event, now. I am Independent.

VIOLET: I will, I will remember. I am ignorant and stupid and I must remember.

   Her eye lights on JACK'S *leaf.*

Oh how nice! Bilbo, I am going into the country, come – (*She corrects herself.*) Will you come into the country with me? Bilbo, remind me, if I forget it, that you have taken your independence.

BILBO: You never forget a fact.

VIOLET: But now I must be able to.

BILBO: Very well, if you do, I will.

VIOLET: And will you come into the country?

BILBO: Of course!

She turns, sees CHAMPION, *is a shade embarrassed.*

VIOLET: Mr Champion – you come too.

CHAMPION: Madam.

VIOLET: And Champion, close the offices for a few days!

CHAMPION: Madam?

VIOLET: Yes yes – let *everybody* have a holiday! (*She leans on* BILBO's *arm.*) I've had the most extraordinary account from Dr Morgan. Jacko's broken out!

Exit VIOLET, BILBO, CHAMPION.
The light goes, foliage is flown in.
Enter JACK. *He calls.*

JACK: Jacko . . .

Enter JACKO. *He is smoking a cigar. He fetches up Front Stage, close to* JACK *but looking out over audience.*

You seem contented.

JACKO: Contented? I could fly. I am immortal.

JACK: Let's see you fly.

JACKO: Now this will surprise you. (*He stretches out his arms and rises on his toes. It is graceful and serious; we half expect it to happen. But he looks sharply at* JACK *and thumps back onto his feet.*) Uh-uh. Human. That's what I am (*contentedly*). Human, Human, Human.

JACK: Not contented then.

JACKO: That's your error.

He takes a turn, smoking, watched by JACK.

Is it going to thunder?

JACK: I don't know.

JACKO *is arrested. He considers* JACK.

JACKO: Hm . . . If you don't make it thunder, you don't make it not.

JACK: You're wrong.

JACKO: I'm right you ignorant concept. It's cause and effect. Hot air rises. Small particles of moisture, dissipate. Small quantities of electricity, accumulate. When there's enough: Thunderbolt.

JACK: Is that a fact?

JACKO: Mm.

JACK: Nature's wonderful. Where did you get that cigar?

JACKO: Penelope brought it out to me. Weren't you there?

JACK: No?

JACKO: It felt as though you were.

JACK: Well yes – You borrowed. Don't you want her?

JACKO: I've got her.

JACK: You're a liar.

JACKO: You were there. You're the liar.

JACK: *I'd* have been there if you'd had her; that's how I know you didn't; liar.

JACKO: Poor old Jack. I didn't say I'd had her. 'Got' her. She loves me.

> JACK *brushes this impatiently aside.*

We're getting married.

JACK: Married——?

JACKO: Yes.

JACK: But – *Married*!

JACKO: That's right! We're going to run a poultry farm!

JACK: A—? . . . You will go back to being what you were . . . You will give up what I've shown you. For a poultry farm?

JACKO: Damned if I will; I'm keeping that.

JACK: Not on a poultry farm.

JACKO: There was no clause excluding poultry farms. On the Seventh Day, I've got it, if I want it. And I do. For my marriage.

JACK (*appalled – patrols front stage staring in horror at the other human faces there*): Oh, the rapacity! . . . What skinflints they've become . . . What terms! This poultry farm – in my Forest?

JACKO: In our half of it.

JACK: A poultry farm! . . . What terms!

The village clock strikes twelve.

Midnight. The Seventh Day's started.

They take up their positions as they did for the 'bargain'.

JACKO: I'm not ungrateful Jack. What you've given me you know; what you've freed me from you can't even imagine.

JACK: All right, all right. I make what terms I can. You want it?

JACKO: Indeed I do.

JACK: All right. Here it is.

Whips out knife. JACKO *starts back.* JACK *laughs a little at the comical misunderstanding.*

Oh it's not for you. Anyone will do.

Reverses knife. JACKO *backs again.*

What's the matter?

JACKO: I don't want that! I want what I borrowed!

JACK: You borrowed me. (*Gravely, warningly.*) Not just a bit of me – so far and no farther – all of me. *Do* you want me?

JACKO: Yes.

JACK: Then you want what I want. You know what I want. (*Slips the knife into* JACKO's *hand. Coaxingly.*) Don't you?

JACKO (*whispers*): *Why?*

JACK: I want it. (*Coaxingly.*) Don't I?

JACKO: They hang you for murder.

JACK: No no, you would be under my protection. Jacko everybody laughs at you. Don't tell me there's nobody you want to kill.

JACKO: No!

Casts knife away. JACK, *furious.*

JACK: You don't want that? Then you'll be wanting these! Your spectacles!

JACKO: No!

JACK (*bitter mirth*): What – you think that you can have it both ways?

    A pause.

JACKO: Yes.

    A pause.

JACK (*aghast*): Jacko!

JACKO: No!

JACK: Jacko!

JACKO: No! (*Backing off.*) Thou shalt not kill!

JACK: Uh?

JACKO: I will not murder!

JACK: But someone's got to be murdered.

JACKO: Then do it yourself.

JACK: I can't murder! I can only kill! Some man must die, some man must do it—! Jacko – !

JACKO: No!

JACK: There's got to be blood!

JACKO: No!

JACK: Then how am I to live?

JACKO: That's your affair.

JACK: Believe me no it's not – it's yours, it's yours—

JACKO: Don't Jack!

JACK: Jacko, don't!

JACKO: Jack!

JACK: Jacko!

JACKO: Please!

JACK: *Please!*

JACKO: You're *mad*!

    A moment's silence. JACK *on his knees, hands clasped beseechingly;* JACKO *stares about him near the end of his tether; his wild gaze focuses on* JACK. *He points.*

I don't know if you're there or not—

JACK: Jacko——!

JACKO: I don't know if this is the Forest or the dark inside of my own skull——

JACK *faces to earth, weeps audibly.*

But I am not going to give up what you've shown me.
Neither am I going to kill. I have decided.

Exit JACKO.

JACK: The *conceit*! 'I have decided'. What – do they think
I am – a relaxation! . . . Do they think that they can call
me, and rouse me, and torment me – and then – send me
back? Do they think I am – a holiday! . . . Oh very well
very well. I must fend for myself. We'll do it the old way.
I will fend, for myself.

He is going, but arrested by a thought.

Unless——

Returns Front Stage. Offers knife, haft first, to audience.

Is there an animal in the House? Someone who will stand
up, for what he wants – a natural man? I am your nature,
and I want it! . . . You sir? You would be under my
protection . . . I am a god! I am a very great god! . . . No?
All – thoughtful? Lot of little Platos are we? (*Sadly.*) There
was a time——

He hears his own phrase. A last hope dawns. Eagerly.

There was a time, when meadow, grove and stream, the
earth, and every common sight, to you did seem apparelled
in celestial light, the glory and the freshness of a dream.
Remember?

No response. A bit desperate.

Oh who will come a Maying oh, a Maying oh, a Maying
oh? Oh who will come a Maying oh, among the woods
. . . so green?

No response.

An hendy happe ychabbe yhent, Ichot from heven it is me
sent, From alle wymen me love is lent and lycht – Remember? (*He dashes furiously into*) Neud amser gwelaf
gweilgi, gweilig moradur hwylfar helli – No? (*Offering
the knife for the last time.*)

Then I'll fend for myself. I'd have preferred it done with

dignity. And you, only do with dignity what you do wittingly. But I'll get it done. Oh believe me.

Dawn breaks.

Enter TREADGOLD *in pyjamas and dressing-gown.* JACK *puts on the spectacles.*

Good morning Cedric.

TREADGOLD: Oh! Good morning Mr Cadence, I didn't see you!

JACK: What's the time?

TREADGOLD: Barely six.

JACK: Barely six. I've got the whole day, haven't I? Will you do something for me?

TREADGOLD: If I can.

JACK: Oh this is all you can do.

TREADGOLD: What then?

JACK: Mark the passage of time for an hour.

TREADGOLD: Er?

JACK: Here's your wife; she'll help you.

Exit JACK, *enter* MRS TREADGOLD, *raincoat over night-gown.*

MRS TREADGOLD: Cedric! I've been looking for you.

TREADGOLD: Yes dear. That was Mr Cadence. He talked very strangely.

MRS TREADGOLD: Cedric.

TREADGOLD: Yes dear?

MRS TREADGOLD: I've been wondering if raising the devil is a suitable hobby for a Christian minister.

TREADGOLD: But Barbara, this is the merest superstition.

MRS TREADGOLD: Well it is in the bible.

TREADGOLD: My little girl. My dear, little, girl.

He pats her hand rather forcibly. She removes it.

MRS TREADGOLD: Oh dear, I've made you angry.

TREADGOLD: Oh how foolish you are. (*Going, stops.*) He asked me to mark the passage of time.

MRS TREADGOLD: How can you do that?

TREADGOLD: I don't know. What *is* the time?

MRS TREADGOLD (*consulting watch*): Seven o'clock.

TREADGOLD: Well let's go in.

 Exit TREADGOLDS. *Bird whistles. Enter* BRACKETS.

BRACKET: How goes it?

MRS BRACKET: Fine. How goes it with you?

BRACKET: Fine. Fine. (*Going.*)

MRS BRACKET: The bees are up early today.

BRACKET (*returning*): Aye they are. Well . . . (*Going.*)

MRS BRACKET: Going to be a scorcher.

BRACKET: Aye it is.

MRS BRACKET: I just met Jacko.

BRACKET: Oh aye . . .? Joy – You sent the letter?

MRS BRACKET: Yes, Stirling.

 They move together.

BRACKET: Look, old girl——

MRS BRACKET: No! 'No Second Thoughts'!

BRACKET: Well why on earth not?

MRS BRACKET: We'll be all right darling. 'We will Both be Happy If We Don't Have Second Thoughts'. Jacko told me.

BRACKET: Jacko!

MRS BRACKET: Just now. He's right darling.

BRACKET: He's wrong!

MRS BRACKET: He's right . . . He warned me you'd be tempted to have second thoughts.

BRACKET: He what?

MRS BRACKET: Well he was right, wasn't he?

 Exit MRS BRACKET.

BRACKET: Joy——! That bloody – interfering – cocky – little – *Jacko*!

 Exits, beating fist into palm. Bird whistles. Broad day.

 Enter GASTON *and* CYNTHIA.

GASTON: What's the matter?

CYNTHIA: Nothing.

GASTON: But 'nothing' cannot be so much the matter.

CYNTHIA: 'Nothing' is.

GASTON: I do not understand.

CYNTHIA: Skip it.

GASTON: Cynthia——

CYNTHIA: If I were you I'd skip it.

GASTON: What! Am I threatened with some awful, innocent insight? But I am terrified!

She looks away, biting her lip.

Aaah . . . It is this ponderous weather . . .

Slips an arm about her shoulders.

CYNTHIA (*wriggles free*): O-o-oh!

GASTON: You are, ashamed?

CYNTHIA: Yes.

GASTON: Cynthia, what you did was nothing wrong.

CYNTHIA: *I* did nothing.

GASTON: Eh bien. What I did, was natural.

CYNTHIA: Was nothing either.

GASTON: You are – disappointed?

CYNTHIA: Please, skip it.

GASTON: Cynthia, I need to know.

CYNTHIA: You do don't you?

GASTON: Did I – embarrass you?

CYNTHIA: Nope. You put me perfectly at ease.

GASTON: Did I – humiliate you?

CYNTHIA: You were tact personified.

GASTON: Did I – hurt you?

CYNTHIA: I didn't feel a thing! I don't know what you took from me but it was something, Gaston, and you gave me nothing for it. You're good at it if that's what you want; but you're light-fingered, Gaston, you're a shop-lifter. And I've something to tell you: you'll never be naked. No never. When you think you're naked Gaston there's a – a lovely pair of trousers and a pearl grey waistcoat and a morning coat! With tails I promise you! . . . You stood in the sunshine. Under that tree. And you took off your shirt. (*She mimes his consciously athletic movement.*) And you took off your slacks. (*Nonchalantly casts aside an imaginary belt.*) And you looked – (*triumphantly*) – respectable!

    GASTON *makes a furious gesture with foot and fist. She stops and looks away, forlorn.*

GASTON: These are very good insults.

CYNTHIA: They're Jacko's not mine.

GASTON: *Jacko!* . . . He said all of that?

CYNTHIA: Yes.

GASTON: And you listened?

CYNTHIA: I laughed; it's funny.

GASTON: Little idiot! . . . Ignorant, mawkish, schoolgirl! . . . Don't you see, he must have been there!

    The bird whistles, the bees murmur, as CYNTHIA *and* GASTON *exit Left and Right. Enter* SERVANTS, HUBERT, GRIEVES *who come forward while the others make the Temple as in Act One. As they work they too are murmuring in tones of indignation and secret pleasure so that the stage is filled with the sound of anger. They centre upon* HUBERT. *Finally,* SECOND SERVANT *comes to* GRIEVES.

SECOND SERVANT: Hey! Someone's raped his sister!

GRIEVES: Raped Marigold?

SECOND SERVANT: Yes.

GRIEVES: That was carrying coals to Newcastle wasn't it?

    A shout of disapproval from the others; they come forward hostile, surrounding HUBERT. GRIEVES *heavily cuts into their babble.*

What's the matter?

    They stop in silence. But HUBERT *steps forward, a leader.*

HUBERT: I knows what's the mater with 'ee, Johnny Grieves. You'm superior . . . (*Turns to others.*) Superior type is Mr Grieves. I 'eerd Mislazra say.

GRIEVES (*pointing to him steadily*): You'll get your face punched; half-wit or not.

A reprobatory murmur dying away; he has re-established his authority.

SECOND SERVANT: It's not a laughing matter, Johnny.

GRIEVES: Of course it's a laughing matter!

YOUNG LABOURER: Young Jacko done it.

GRIEVES: Young Jacko? . . . No-o-o.

HUBERT: Oh? P'raps you knows of someone else in these parts answerin' to 'is description? Wearin' leaves? Leaves about 'im?

GRIEVES: O-oh . . . that's it . . . young gentleman takes his holiday seriously . . . where is she?

HUBERT: 'Er's 'oam. An' 'er's terrible bashed about!

OLD LABOURER (*uneasy to* HUBERT): Look 'ere my boy, you tell Miz Lazra when 'er comes.

GRIEVES: Oh no. You tell the Police. It's criminal is rape.

OLD LABOURER: You knows as well as I. 'Tis past performin' to rape Marigold. 'Er's ready-raped. Speakin' plainly.

HUBERT: 'Er's dirty, if that's what you means!

GRIEVES: It makes no difference what she is. You tell the Police.

HUBERT: Nor P'lice neither! (*Backs Upstage, dominating them.*) P'lice hereabouts is Colonel Garside. And Colonel Garside 'e be like canary bird with Mistress! Gentry never bothered wi' Marigold, not serious – 'Er's too dirty! But little joke, little joke to finish off 'is week 'er's all right for that – dirty or not! (*Pointing to* GRIEVES.) You or me we bashes a young woman *that's* grimnal! Young gentleman does same – specially if 'is name be *Cadence* 'ereabouts——! That's 'igh spirits! Like – knockin' p'liceman's 'elmet off! (*He croons, lost*) Like – like – 'ittin' I in face with bloody great fist! Bloody great 'ard fist . . . 'Acause your cartridges be wet; 'acause pike 'as etten troutlings – but 'e won't 'ave pike out of there oh no 'e likes to see 'un dash . . . 'cause 'ay be wet 'cause it be rainin'; 'cause apples do be poor an' small an' wormy . . . No, I bain't fetchin' no P'lice.

A murmur of astonished admiration, approval.

GRIEVES: Well where have you been keeping your wits?

HUBERT: I 'as a secret place for they.

Enter TREADGOLD, MRS TREADGOLD.

TREADGOLD: Good evening; Good evening; Good evening Sam; Good evening. Is everything ready?

GRIEVES (*flatly*): Yes sir.

> TREADGOLD *goes right,* MRS TREADGOLD *left. Enter* GASTON *and* BRACKET *who join* TREADGOLD, CYNTHIA *and* MRS BRACKET *who join his wife.*

HUBERT: No I be goin' to find thyk Jacko. An I be goin' to learn 'ee somethin' as 'ee needs to know.

> *Bird whistles. Light thickens towards evening.* TREADGOLD *says to audience:*

TREADGOLD: There's rather a nasty spirit abroad in our little community. However, I expect Miss Lazara will put it down.

Enter VIOLET *and* BILBO, *followed by* CHAMPION.

VIOLET: So sorry you have had to wait. We came by *steam-train*! So exciting – pistons and couplings, slappety-slap – I'd thought they were extinct but not at all – one sees them everywhere! (*To* BILBO.) The atmosphere seems tense? Lady Cynthia! Are you still happy?

CYNTHIA (*deliberately wooden, holding out hand*): Thank you for having me.

VIOLET: Oh. Well go by steam-train. (*Holding* CYNTHIA'*s hand looks towards* GASTON.) Not to be compared with diesel as a means of traction naturally. But so much slower. (*Glances fondly at* BILBO *who looks conscious.*)

CYNTHIA: Monsieur Dupont will not be travelling with me.

VIOLET: Oh. Mrs Bracket – (*takes her hand and, failing to find* BRACKET *on the end of it*) – but where's?

MRS BRACKET: My husband and I have separated Miss Lazara.

VIOLET: Oh. Well if that's what you want. Both of you.

Mrs Treadgold—! (*Indicating knitting bag.*) What are you engaged upon?

MRS TREADGOLD: Nothing. I've finished Cedric's cardigan.

VIOLET: Ah . . . (*To* BILBO.) One feels quite lost without one's knitting. Knit something for Mr Cubit. Bilbo, would like a – Fair Isle cardigan.

BILBO (*charmingly*): That would be, delightful.

VIOLET (*to* MRS TREADGOLD): There now—(*Sweeps across to the men.*) Monsieur Dupont—! What have you done?

GASTON (*harshly*): Insufficient.

VIOLET: You astonish me. I don't suppose she'll go. But if she does take the same train – Oh I do recommend them. Mr Bracket – what superlative weather!

BRACKET: Glad you think so. It's ruined your barley.

VIOLET: Oh. Can't you give it to the cows?

BRACKET: I suppose so, if it's mulched.

VIOLET (*generously*): Then *mulch* it! Mr Treadgold—! (*Sotto.*) Whatever is the *matter* . . .?

    TREADGOLD, *whispers.*

That was carrying coals to Newcastle wasn't it? Where *is* Jacko? And Lady Penelope? And Dr Morgan?

BRACKET: Looking for him.

VIOLET: It's the early bird that catches the worm. (*To* BILBO.) Good heavens I'm colloquial. (*To the generality.*) I understand we're all enchanted by the resurrected Jacko. (*To* TREADGOLD.) Does he turn up here himself or do we all look for him?

TREADGOLD: He should turn up himself.

GASTON: I think we'll have to look for him.

BRACKET: Morgan thinks he's off his head.

GASTON: I am not so sure.

VIOLET: What nonsense! He's come into his inheritance, that's all! (*To* BILBO.) Poor Morgan's jealous, though he doesn't know it. But what can be the matter with these lumps? (*To* TREADGOLD, *indicating his stick.*) What is that?

TREADGOLD (*apologetic*): Oh. The token punishment.

VIOLET (*smiling*.) Ah! (*Takes it. Smile goes.*) Oh. That is hardly token. Oh no I can't have that . . . Put them down please.

They stubbornly look back at her.

Put them down.

They are dropped.

(*She smiles again.*) We'll find him. We'll chastise him just a little, because he's happy. We'll have a lovely supper altogether, and I'll make two announcements. (*Takes* BILBO'*s arm*.) I'll make the first one now; I am going to return this place to Mr Cadence. I always *meant* to . . . The second I shall keep till supper. Oh I haven't introduced . . . This is Mr Bilbo Cubit . . .

Hastily she sweeps away with him and CHAMPION *and Exit.*

YOUNG LABOURER: No fool like an old fool.

Re-enter VIOLET, *followed by* BILBO *and* CHAMPION.

VIOLET: What imbecile said that?

No answer.

BILBO: Violet——

VIOLET:——No! . . . What *cretin*?

No answer.

BILBO: Darling——

VIOLET:——Don't! By God I'll sack you all——!

BILBO: Violet——

VIOLET: You are all dismissed! Away you shall go! Out of your houses——!

GRIEVES (*with satisfaction*): Well then. There's nothing more to wait for, is there?

They go.

VIOLET: Stop!

But Exit SERVANTS, GRIEVES, HUBERT, *also* BRACKET, GASTON, TREADGOLD.

What the devil has been going on here?

It begins to be dark. Peremptory:

Bilbo, come with me.

BILBO: No thank you, Violet.

VIOLET: What the devil——?

BILBO: You asked me to remind you. I'm reminding you.

VIOLET: Bilbo!

BILBO: I'll be in the library.

Exit BILBO. *It is moonlight.*

MR TREADGOLD's *stick is prominent.*

VIOLET: Pick that up.

CHAMPION *does so.*

Come with me.

Exit VIOLET, CHAMPION, *the* WOMEN.

Enter PENELOPE. *She calls.*

PENELOPE: Jacko!

A VOICE (*off, Left*): Here I am.

PENELOPE: Darling?

Enter JACKO, *Right.*

JACKO: Did you call me darling?

PENELOPE: Jacko. Come into the House; there's Hell to pay.

JACKO: No. There isn't. (*He sits.*) You haven't got another of those cigars have you?

PENELOPE: In the House.

JACKO: What's the time then?

PENELOPE: Ten to midnight.

JACKO: I'll be in in ten minutes.

PENELOPE: You're barmy, Jacko.

JACKO: Don't say that; it's unlucky. (*But looking up and seeing her unease, he pulls her down beside him.*) Listen, when I come in, we will be happy.

PENELOPE: Yes.

JACKO: No, I mean it. At midnight I will bring you: safety and ecstasy, freedom and peace, the Lion *and* the Lamb.

PENELOPE: Is that a promise?

JACKO: Yes.

PENELOPE: Shall we have children Jacko?

JACKO: Six,

PENELOPE: How d'you know?

JACKO: I fancy six.

PENELOPE: They'll be beautiful.

JACKO: Yes. And good.

PENELOPE: Good children.

JACKO: Yes. And beautiful. We're going to have it both ways.

PENELOPE (*gently*): Jacko, no one has it both ways.

JACKO: If that were true it wouldn't be worth having. And it is. I'm going to get it for you. Will you go in now?

PENELOPE: No.

JACKO: I want you to go in.

PENELOPE: I'm going to stay here.

JACKO: If you love me you'll go in.

    She goes. Chidingly.

Don't be frightened.

PENELOPE: Come with me then.

JACKO (*lightly*): I have to say goodbye to Jack.

    She stares. His smile goes.

(*Steadily.*) To say goodbye to Jack.

PENELOPE: You do mean metaphorically?

    He hesitates.

Jacko?

    He hesitates.

Darling?

JACKO: Yes.

    Thunder clap and lightning flash. In the ensuing moment of blindness, PENELOPE *is replaced by* MORGAN. JACKO's *back is turned. The wind is blowing and the moonlight travels across the stage.*

MORGAN: Jacko!

    JACKO *turns and we see that it is* JACK, *still wearing* JACKO's *spectacles.*

You fool! Come into the House. Come into the House and I will do what I can for you.

JACK *turns his back again.*

You think because I am a man of mind I cannot know the nature of your suffering. That's wrong. Because I am I do. For you are like me, Jacko – *me*! Except that you're a fool. You've sided with the body, with simple, baying matter, and you hope for happiness.

JACK *looks at him, smiles, and looks away.*

Attend to me!

JACK *looks mildly back.*

Matter scrutinized by mind becomes a sort of whirling grit, is it not so?

JACK *gravely nods.*

In which what you would call a man is a momentary complexity, only well expressed in figures. One, two, three, four, five, six, seven, eight, nine and nought. That's the Life of Nature and compared with that, Death's rowdy! And this knowledge is what mind is. And mind is all that man is. There are not many men. Accept. Be quiet. And be one!

JACK *begins to laugh.* MORGAN *advances on him.*

Oh arrogate no special fitness to yourself because you call your figure 'love'. I know your 'love', is a figure!

JACK, *still laughing silent laughter, approaching* MORGAN *takes off his spectacles.* MORGAN *stares.*

Jacko?

Enter JACKO.

JACKO (*desperately*): Jack!

MORGAN (*amazed*): Jacko?

JACKO (*desperately –* JACK *has his knife out*): Jack!

MORGAN (*staring at* JACKO, *backing from* JACK): Jacko——!

JACKO (*desperately*): Jack——!

Lightning flash. Blindness, in which thunderclap. Afterwards MORGAN *on his back.* JACK *bending over him, his knife crimson to the hilt.*

JACKO: *Why?*

JACK: *Trust* me!

Lightning flash. SERVANTS, GASTON, BRACKET, TREADGOLD, GRIEVES, HUBERT, *have entered and are frozen in attitudes of horror glaring down at* MORGAN'S *body. They carry rough sticks.* JACK *and* JACKO *crouch towards them,* JACKO *grasped by* JACK, *forced to grasp the knife.*

GRIEVES: He's dead!

BRACKET: Dr Morgan!

GASTON: The good man!

TREADGOLD: The thinker!

JACK: How we loved him!

CHORUS: How we *loved* him!

TREADGOLD: Who *did* it?

JACKO: *I* did!

For the first time they look up. A roar.

CHORUS: Jacko!

JACK: How we *hate* him!

CHORUS (*roaring, rush at* JACKO):—Hate him!

JACKO *drops the knife, turns, runs. As he goes,* JACK *puts out a foot and trips him. As he falls, the* CHORUS *is upon his fallen body with their sticks, shouting, the bees roaring, the moonlight scudding.* TREADGOLD *stands and covers his face.* JACK *seizes* HUBERT, *spins him round as in a dance, crying:*

JACK: The boot! The boot! The boot!

He spins HUBERT *into the mêlée. We see* HUBERT *kicking.* JACK *retrieves his knife. Triumphant, joyful.*

Murder.

Instant stillness. Enter VIOLET *with* CHAMPION, MRS TREADGOLD, MRS BRACKET, CYNTHIA.

VIOLET: In God's name, what——

Lightning. Blindness. JACK *has vanished.* CHAMPION, *stricken, is walking back towards* VIOLET *and the women.*

CHAMPION: Madam, come away. This is no place for you.

VIOLET: No? Then whose place is it?

The thunderclap belonging to the lightning rumbles a shade less close. CHORUS *stands still and hangdog about* JACKO – 'Post coitum . . .' VIOLET *goes and looks at* MORGAN. *Turns away her head. Walks towards* JACKO.

BRACKET (*mouth trembling*): Ja-Jack-Jacko——

She walks on. The CHORUS *opens. She stops. We see* JACKO *for the first time; his face is a red mask.*

VIOLET: *Cover* them with something! *Cover* them!

Every man present takes off his jacket, and they are covered. Feeble lightning flash.

BRACKET (*croaking*): We thought – we ought – He tripped and——

VIOLET: Tripped! You – *animals*!

OLD LABOURER *detaches himself from* CHORUS.

OLD LABOURER: 'T weren't we as put 'un up to it, Mizlazra. 'Twere gentry.

Exit, silently SERVANTS, GRIEVES, HUBERT, OLD LABOURER *saying:*

'Tis always gentry.

Receding thunder.

VIOLET: Lady Cynthia, Monsieur Dupont, I am closing my House. Please make it convenient to leave tomorrow.

Exit CYNTHIA *and* GASTON.

Mrs Treadgold, look after your husband.

Exit TREADGOLDS.

Bracket, phone for the Police. Make them put you through to the Chief Constable. Use my name.

Exit BRACKET, MRS BRACKET *after a moment following.*

Bilbo?

CHAMPION: I think he said the library.

VIOLET *emits a little sound between contempt and laughter.*

CHAMPION *opens his mouth, shuts it.*

VIOLET: Yes?

CHAMPION: No.

VIOLET (*her voice is high and tremulous, but she controls herself*): Is it a business matter?

CHAMPION: I don't know.

He can't get into his jacket. VIOLET *helps him.*

VIOLET: Give me the facts then and I'll tell you.

CHAMPION: I understand that Mr Cubit's independence rests in Quantox Preferential.

VIOLET: Yes.

CHAMPION: It's not a sound stock.

VIOLET: No.

CHAMPION: It wouldn't stand a lot of selling.

VIOLET: No.

CHAMPION: Our Holding Company owns fifty-one per cent of Galt Marine.

VIOLET: And Galt Marine owns fifty-one per cent of Fortunas and Fortunas hold half a million Quantox. (*Sadly smiling.*) Did you think I had forgotten?

CHAMPION: I beg your pardon.

VIOLET: It is a business matter. Sell.

CHAMPION: Madam?

VIOLET: Sell.

CHAMPION: And . . . Mr Cubit . . .?

VIOLET: A dream. Pretence. Play-acting. Sell.

CHAMPION (*softly as though* JACKO *and* MORGAN *might overhear*): They must have had . . . the most ferocious quarrel.

VIOLET: No. Poor Morgan. (*Crossing.*) No. (*She takes the coat from* JACKO*'s face, masking it from the audience.*)

CHAMPION *who has followed turns away his head but she steadily looks and carefully replaces the coat.*

Poor boy. (*Wondering, awed, envious.*) He thought, he was, the *real thing* . . . What courage!

Exit VIOLET *and* CHAMPION. *The stage is left empty. Perhaps we shall see the god again? Distant thunder rumbles softly. Instead, it rains, and this rain should be as naturalistic as possible and as beautiful as rain sometimes is.*

CURTAIN